The Disappearance of Susan Powell

Pete Dirk

Published by Trellis Publishing, 2021.

While every precaution has been taken in the preparation of this book, the publisher assumes no responsibility for errors or omissions, or for damages resulting from the use of the information contained herein.

THE DISAPPEARANCE OF SUSAN POWELL

First edition. July 11, 2021.

ISBN: 979-8224627714

Written by Pete Dirk.

THE DISAPPEARANCE OF SUSAN POWELL

PETE DIRK

The Ripples That Emerge From Murder

Murder is rarely simple. But the complex strands of criminality that surround the almost certain death of Susan Powell serve to obscure the reality of a very tragic situation. Through a series of related causes, a mother, a father, a grandfather, an uncle and – worst of all – two young children have died prematurely.

In some of those cases, the circumstances of the victims' deaths have been truly horrific. It is approaching a decade now since Susan, the first of the extended family to lose her life, disappeared, presumed dead. But the causes of her demise reach back much further in time.

The principle actors in this morbid drama are Susan, her husband Josh, his father Steven and brother Michael. The two youngest victims are Charles Powell, who was seven at the time and his brother Brad, just five years old when he died in appalling circumstances.

Josh and Susan were married just after the turn of the millennium, with the attractive twenty year old recording in her journal: 'I just feel incredibly lucky to have Josh.' But those early days of married bliss did not last for long. By 2008, the tone of her entries had changed considerably. 'If I die,' she wrote, 'it may not be an accident even if it looks like one. Take care of my boys.' By then, her husband Josh was two years into an affair with a woman who lived not far from their West Valley City, Utah, home. His personality was a controlling one. He limited his wife's access to the internet and monitored her phone calls. Her spending was restricted. The attitude he displayed towards his boys was similarly controlling. Josh's behaviour was a cause of serious concern. But as we said at the outset, murder is rarely simple, and while on the one hand Susan was growing increasingly worried about her husband's demeanour, the two were still trying to conceive their third child.

Perhaps it was Susan's deeply held religious beliefs that contributed to her continued willingness to give the marriage more time.

Susan and Josh, who was five years older than his wife, had married in Portland, Oregon during April 2001, then moved to West Valley City, which is a suburb of Salt Like City, in 2004. Susan was a cosmetologist, working in the beauty industry and Josh had a series of jobs following his time in college, where he acquired a bachelor's degree in business. Despite his qualifications, he found it difficult to hold down a job, but never let a lack of employment or income curtail his spending. He was exuberant with his expenditure – as long as it was on himself. While he was determined to limit his wife's independence, he built up large debts of his own.

This financial instability was certainly a factor as their marriage began to struggle. By 2007, about the time that he began his affair with another woman, he needed to file for bankruptcy, declaring debts of over $200000. A further cause of the anger between the two was that, although both were regular and committed church goers, Susan wanted to tythe 10% of their income to their church. Josh refused, preferring to add the sum to the amount he lavished on himself.

Another concern was Josh's violence. Such was the worry this was instilling into the young mother that, in 2009, she filmed their house, recording the damage he had caused during a fit of temper. She hid the film away with her journal and a secret will, which included the statement 'I want it documented that there is extreme turmoil in our marriage.'

By the end of that year Susan would be gone, presumed dead. At this time, her son Charles was four years old, and Braden was just two. Susan and the boys attended their regular church service on December 6th 2009, and were also visited by a neighbour who reported that she had left their home at around 5.00pm. All had seemed well.

Christmas was not far away, and the weather was preparing for it. Snow lay on the ground and the chill in the air saw the temperature reaching only the low teens. According to Josh's story, what happened next was that he returned home and announced that he had planned a surprise camping trip for the boys. He would take them off for a night in the wilds.

The story is bizarre. To take a toddler and a very young boy camping, leaving late at night, is a strange thing to do. To do so in freezing conditions is stranger still. In fact, it borders on the irresponsible. Later, Charlie, the older son, confirmed that this trip had indeed taken place. He younger brother also, in his own way, gave evidence of it. He drew a picture of three people in a van. When he was asked who was in his picture, he explained it was he and his brother, their daddy, and that mommy was 'in the trunk.'

Charlie too later said that when they arrived Daddy and Mommy had gone into some caves to look for crystals. Only Daddy had come out, and his mom was still there, looking for these jewels. Later, he told his maternal grandparents that 'Mommy is dead.'

However, according to Josh, he had taken the boys alone, and when he returned home the next day, Susan was gone. He said that the last time he had seen of his wife she was sleeping. It was just after midnight on December 7th, he had kissed her goodbye and then had taken the boys off to Simpson Springs, which lay about two to three hours away.

In fact, friends had reported to the police that the whole family were missing early in the morning of December 7th. The police attended their house, and fearing something like carbon monoxide poisoning, had forced their way in. Inside they found nobody, although in a downstairs room two fans were on, drying an area of bloodied carpet. Later, that blood would be identified as belonging to Susan and an unidentified male.

The first thought was that the whole family had indeed gone, but when Josh returned he was taken to the police station, where he made his report about finding Susan out when he returned. He showed no evidence of concern or worry about the whereabouts of his missing wife.

In fact, he seemed pretty sure that she would not be returning. Right from the start, he cancelled regular sessions she held with a chiropractor; he ended and cashed in her retirement policies, and, investigators discovered, he had taken out a $1.5 million insurance policy on his wife. Then Charlie revealed more information – he told a teacher at his school that his mother was dead.

Josh Powell withdrew his children from their day-care, and was reported to have spoken with his co-workers about the best way to hide a body in an abandoned mineshaft. He was interviewed by CBS news, who directly asked him whether he was responsible for his wife's disappearance. 'I've never even hurt her,' he replied. 'People who know me know that I could never hurt Susan.'

Meanwhile, police continued to search for the missing woman. They visited Simpson Springs, but could find no evidence that anybody had camped in the place Josh identified. They were concerned about the man, about his almost nonchalant attitude to his missing wife and his lack of interest in helping police to locate her.

Eventually, the probability grew that Susan was more than just missing, and was in fact dead. Josh was inevitably a suspect on their list, but they had no evidence to back up their suspicions. Then suddenly Josh up sticked, and took the boys to live in his father's house several hundreds of miles away in Washington State. Initially, it seemed as though the trip was just an extended holiday, but when news reached him that investigators planned to question him further, he returned to his home along with his brother, Michael, packed their belongings and moved in permanently with his father, Steven, in Puyallup, Washington. By January 2010, he had moved out of Utah for good.

Steven had, in fact, always been a shadowy figure in the background of their morbid marriage. He had displayed an unhealthy and inappropriate, if not exactly illegal, interest in Susan right from their first meeting. He would talk about things not normally said between a woman and her father in law; he liked to video her, especially when she was scantily clad. When the media first became interested in Susan's disappearance, and began to interview members of the wider family, he claimed that his daughter in law had actually run off with a man from St George, Utah, who had disappeared at around the same time.

Josh added to the picture he was attempting to create of himself being the victim in all this. His wife, he told his new neighbours and the media, was mentally ill, and was 'extremely unstable.'

For eighteen months, matters progressed little, and the media attention began to fade. Two boys would grow up without their mother, but other pressing news took her story firstly into the background and finally out of the attention of all but those closest to her.

Then, in August 2011, matters suddenly came a head once more. Firstly, although the case was no longer at the forefront of the police's interest, nevertheless they continued to work on leads as they arose. They received a tip off that an abandoned mineshaft in Ely, Nevada could be of interest. The site was two hundred miles away from West Valley, but still the police followed up the lead, although it came to nothing.

Then, two days later, a remembrance service was held for Susan. It was now twenty months since she had disappeared. At the event, the boys' two grandfathers fell into an argument. Accusations were clearly made, and Steven Powell was reported as shouting at Susan's father, Chuck Cox, that he was 'a liar.'

Josh Powell is still, at this point, a person of interest to the police. But their concerns are spreading wider, and they begin to take seriously reports that Steven Powell was infatuated with his son's wife. On August 25th 2011, investigators secure a search warrant to scour Steven's house, looking for any clues that might link him to Susan's disappearance. They come up with nothing, but make a different and very disturbing discovery.

On Steven's computers are found inappropriate videos and stills of children. The shots and recordings include film of his young neighbours bathing. A month later Steven is formally arrested for possession of pornographic images of children. The next day, an injunction is given declaring that neither Steven nor Josh can publish any material from Susan's journals, which they now have in their possession. The drip feed of character assassination with which they had been attacking her character is forced to stop. This event, though, coincides with Steven Powell's claims that his daughter in law had made sexual advances towards him that were 'beyond the pale.' And on 28th September, 2011, the boys are finally removed out of the home and control of their father. They are instead placed with Susan's parents, Chuck and Judy. The reason is that sexually explicit material has been recovered from the home in which they had been resident.

As bad as that is, another reason for removing the boys is at the back of the authority's thinking. Always a person about whom they had doubts, Josh's involvement in Susan's disappearance, or knowledge of what happened to her on that night in December 2009, is becoming of greater interest to them. On September 14th, a week before Steven was charged, they had received another tip off, this time directing them to a shallow grave some thirty miles from Simpson Springs. This is Topaz Mountain, and the discovery they make there leads police to believe that they may have finally located Susan's body. However, confusion did reign. Some reports said that, despite digging several inches down, they could find no remains. Police had been led to the specific spot when attention by cadaver dogs suggested something present. Some suggestions were that it could be an ancient burial site that had attracted the animals, but local experts ruled this out as a possibility. Nevertheless, it was yet another piece of a jigsaw that would lead to the picture of Josh Powell as a killer. It is a tragedy of the greatest proportions that the final pieces of that jigsaw should be so mired in innocent blood.

In fact, the police's interest in Josh had been quietly growing for some time. Although he retained the full support of his brother Michael, as well as his father, another member of the Powell family was much less trusting of her sibling.

Jennifer Graves began to have doubts about her brother's actions. Initially, her sister Alina shared her concerns, although in time she began to be of the opinion that her brother was being harassed. One of the reasons that Jennifer had her suspicions came from his reactions to Susan's disappearance. Sisters know when they have volatile siblings, and that certainly applied in Jennifer's case, but she was nonplussed by the apparent calm her brother displayed about his wife – his sons' mother's (and it cannot surely get bigger than that) – disappearance. She began to suspect that Josh knew more than he was letting on. Perhaps her father and her other brother, Michael, did too.

She decided to fly Washington, with her husband, and to confront them.

'It suddenly occurred to me,' she said, 'I wonder if the police would back me up?' They did agree for her to wear a wire which they could monitor from a van down the street. A series of codewords were established so that police could intervene quickly if anything started to go wrong.

'It was the scariest thing I've ever done' she said of entering the house wearing a wire. 'I shoved him (her brother) into the bathroom and I was, like, tell me where her body is. We need to have a funeral.' Even the anger of his sibling, though, had no impact on Josh.

'He was so deadpan, there was no emotion, there was nothing,' said Jennifer. Her father was more emotional. He his daughter out of the house, calling her a 'bitch'.

But despite all of this, Josh retained access rights to his sons. Remember, whatever we think about the authorities allowing for this, he had still to be charged with any crime. With his sons now living hundreds of miles away with his parents in law, he rented a house near them. The agreement was that he had visitation rights, as long as those visits were supervised by a social worker. Under these circumstances, normally such meetings take place in public, at a Macdonald's or such like. But Josh decided he would have the children come to his house.

Matters took on an even darker turn on February 1st 2012. Police were continuing to study the computers they had taken from Steven's house, and they made some findings which, while not as severe as say the film of the neighbour's young daughters found on Steven's computer, still raised concerns. The police statement said that these images and information 'specifically related to the children's welfare.'

The outcome was that Josh was ordered to undertake a psycho-sexual evaluation and a polygraph test. He had avoided for two years all but the briefest comments about Susan's disappearance and his own private life, now it seemed as though details were bound to emerge.

To Chuck and Judy, such a move raised a red flag – in fact, a hug, waving warning banner. If these evaluations and tests had to happen, then Josh must have further restrictions placed on his access to their grandchildren. The couple had already started the process of filing for complete custody of the boys, but processes are slow, and this latest development signalled danger. Chuck summed it up:

'Whenever he (Josh) gets pushed,' he said, 'something bad happens.' He warned the police and child protection services: 'If Josh gets cornered, he could kill the boys.'

Judy sensed something was wrong the day before the social worker came to collect the boys to take them on their supervised visit to their father. But when Judy raised her concerns, the social worker could do nothing: 'I have to take the boys,' she said. Josh had his rights, and even though he was a suspect in his wife's disappearance, and had been found with inappropriate information or images of children on his computer, there was nothing that could be done.

But grandparents have a sixth sense about their grandchildren, and to Chuck and Judy it was clear that something would happen on the visit. Judy described her anxiety as being a premonition of disaster.

In the light of what happened next, such a position was understandable. But, even though the sensationalist elements of the media threw their hands up in horror, at that point Josh had been charged with nothing and had not even been arrested. As Chuck said: 'Boys need their father.' It is easy to be wise after the event.

It was February 5th 2012 and the awful fears of the Cox family were realised. The social worker arrived on time, and Josh was waiting at the door of his small but nearby rented home. He opened the door a little, and the boys rushed inside, glad to see Daddy as much as they enjoyed living with their Grandad and Grandma.

The social worker did a double take, as her nose registered the unmistakeable odour of petrol leaking from the home. But that was as far as she got. Powell slammed the door behind her, and locked it. Although she banged hard to get inside, there was no way to get past the door. In desperation she telephoned her bosses at the town hall.

Meanwhile, inside the house, Josh had apparently lost his mind. Whether to try to spare them the death that was about to come, or just as a result of an emotional collapse we will never know, but Josh grabbed the boys and began to hack at them with a hatchet. They were discovered later with deep gouges in their heads, neck and shoulders. Imagine the fear and disbelief as their daddy hurt them so badly. It is impossible to conceive of such cruelty, but that is what happened.

Their agony was, though, relatively short lived. Josh had clearly planned for his sons' arrival. The house was so full with accelerant that pockets of the fumes were mixing with the oxygen in the air, forming small but deadly fuel that needed just a spark to ignite them. The father gave that spark, and an explosion ripped through the house. One can only trust that death for the two young boys was instant, and that they did not have to bear the agony of burning.

Later, firefighters told the media that it was unlikely that they would have known anything about what happened to them. The power of the explosion would suck all surrounding oxygen forcibly into it, and unconsciousness would be almost instantaneous. If the wounds from the hatchet had not already killed them, then at least they would be out of pain by the time either the explosion itself or the powerful fire that followed ensured that they, along with their father, were dead.

We will never know for sure whether Joshua Powell killed his wife, simply knew of her death and where she was left, or in fact that he was innocent of any involvement, however unlikely that seems. But we do know that he murdered his two sons, perhaps in a state of temporary insanity, perhaps out of spite that, if he could not have them then nobody would. He also killed himself.

Meanwhile the social worker was in momentary shock at the power and surprise of the explosion.

She called 911. 'He exploded the house,' she said. The operator replies, 'Do you know if anyone is in the house?' The social worker responds with the worse news possible. 'Yes, there was a man and two children. I just dropped off the children and he wouldn't let me in the door.' She has remained, in the circumstances, calm, a professional demeanour staying in place. But then, as the full horror enters her mind, the equilibrium shatters and her voice rises in anguish. 'He blew up the house and the kids!'

One of Powell's new neighbour's, Ryan Mickle, said of the explosion: 'It shook my house and then I ran outside and the whole house on fire almost immediately.'

There was no chance that the fire could be an accident. The Pierce County Sherriff's Department's Ed Troyer made that clear. 'This wasn't an accident,' he said. 'This was Josh Powell, who we believe killed his kids and himself, dead in the fire.'

'He grabbed the kids, locked her out of the house and immediately, the house went up in flames,' he continued. 'We believe that the house fire went up so fast that accelerants were used.'

The Pierce County Sheriff, Paul Pastor, was equally clear that murders had been committed. 'This is a terrible act of murder involving two young children,' he explained. 'Let's call it like it is. Let's call it a horrible murder, because that's exactly what we have here.

And any lingering notion of a tragic accident disappeared when it was revealed that Powell had sent an email to his attorney just ten minutes before the explosion. 'I'm sorry. Goodbye,' the message read.

When their deaths became public, students, parents and teachers held a candlelit vigil at the boys' school.

Jennifer (Josh's sister) recalls hearing the news. 'The boys were gone,' she told a reporter for the documentary 'Crime Watch Daily.' 'Josh had blown up the house. I was just numb.'

For Chuck and Judy Cox it is impossible to imagine the suffering they went through. Their daughter was missing, and had to be presumed dead. Now, as surrogate parents to her sons, they had lost two more children.

Memories of the two boys, just five and seven at their deaths, mix happiness with deep sorrow.

Chuck Cox remembers: 'Charlie was a scientist. Kids in the first grade called him "the Scientist"'

Judy Cox: 'He said such nice things, like "I love you Grandma. I'm so glad you're here.'

They suffered guilt that they had allowed the boys to go on that final trip (they could no other) mixed with despair at their loss and anger at the members of the family into which their daughter had married.

But they had, and still experience, further misgivings about the whole situation.

The Cox's feel that Child Protection Services were in the wrong. After their grandsons' deaths, they contacted an attorney, Anne Bremner. 'It defies logic that they wanted to unify that man with those kids,' she argued. 'And they said in deposition that they believed he had killed his wife. They (child protection services) basically took those kids by the hand like lambs to slaughter.' The grieving grandparents launched legal action against the local child protection department, arguing negligence on their part.

The saga, though, was still not complete. In May of that year Steven Powell was sentenced to prison for counts of voyeurism regarding the images and photographs he took of the two young girls who lived next door. He spent the rest of his life in and out of prison on related charges, including a short time for failing to attend treatment sessions for sexual deviancy. Powell later died of natural causes. The deserved stresses of his later life most probably contributed to his demise.

For Jennifer Powell, matters were still not closed. As wicked as her brother and father had been, they were still family. She had also lost a sister in law that she liked, and two nephews she adored. The suffering is unlikely to ever completely pass. She strongly suspected that her other brother, Michael, was inculcated in the crime. Indeed, her feeling, and increasingly that of the police, was that it was Michael who had committed the murder while Josh and the boys were camping. Possibly it had even happened before, while the boys slept. She believes that it may have been he who had helped Josh to load Susan's body into their van.

Just over a year after his brother's death, Michael filed notion to claim the $1.5 million life insurance policy that Josh had taken out. His claim did not succeed, and in the end it seemed as though all became too much. Guilt? Sadness? Remorse? He moved to Minneapolis for Graduate School and committed suicide. Within three years, his father was dead too.

Susan was officially declared dead, in line with the law in Utah, on December 6th, 2014, the fifth anniversary of her disappearance. Maybe the guilty ones had paid the ultimate price, but the innocent continue to suffer

THE MURDER OF AMY ALLWINE

JESSI DIXON

15

In May 2016, a team of hackers cracked into a site on the dark web – and unknowingly uncovered evidence that would eventually help investigators with the FBI solve the murder of a woman named Amy Allwine.

"If you want to kill someone, or to beat the shit out of him, we are the right guys," read the homepage of Besa Mafia, a website that was supposedly affiliated with an Albanian organized crime ring. In exchange for bitcoin, they claimed they would arrange beatings and even assassinations. The site had appealed to many potential clients, including a user named "dogdaygod."

The FBI determined that "dogdaygod" was responsible for arranging the murder of Amy Allwine, a church-going Midwestern woman. "Dogdaygod" wanted the slaying to "look like an accident," according to the emails sent to Besa Mafia. The user claimed Amy Allwine "tore my family apart by sleeping with my husband, and is stealing clients from my business."

However, this portrayal of Amy Allwine didn't fit with the victim's life. The 43 year old dog trainer ran her own business in a suburb outside of St. Paul, Minnesota. She'd met her husband, Stephen, at a Christian college, and the couple had continued to pursue their dedication to their faith as active members of a local congregation of the United Church of God. Stephen even served as church elder, providing marriage counselling services to couples who were struggling to stay together. The couple even raised an adopted son.

"Amy was the most motivating person, she was the most positive person," said Jennifer Waters, one of Amy's dog training students. "She had nothing but good things to say about anybody."

Friends and family described Amy as a loving, devoted mother and a compassionate, dedicated friend. She seemed hardly to be the kind of woman "dogdaygod" insisted that she was, but it looked like someone was trying to have her killed.

In July 2016, a woman who called herself Jane sent Amy Allwine the first of two untraceable emails containing threats and insults. Jane said Amy was a "fat bitch" who had destroyed the woman's marriage, and more disturbingly, threatened Amy's family and her son – using details that clearly gave the impression that Jane had the Allwines under surveillance.

"Here is how you can save your family," read Jane's initial email. "Commit suicide."

The email went on to assure Amy that if she did not comply with the sender's instructions to kill herself, she would "slowly see things taken away from you, and each time you will know that you could have stopped it." It also included a list of suggested methods Amy could employ to carry out the grisly deed.

Around the same time, the FBI reached out to the Cottage Grove police department, advising them of the murder-for-hire plot where some unknown user was planning to pay virtual currency to have Amy killed. The police met with the Allwines and recommended they step up their home security. And they did – Stephen even received a permit to carry a handgun on August 10, and purchased a 9mm Springfield XDS to protect his wife.

But just months later, that same gun would be used to kill her.

Murder for hire

The plot to kill Amy appears to have originated on Valentine's Day, according to a timeline later pieced together by investigators from the FBI, Cottage Grove police, and the Minnesota Bureau of Criminal Apprehension. On February 14, 2016, "dogdaygod" attempted to pay $5,000 to have Amy Allwine killed in a car crash.

The user provided Besa Mafia with plenty of information to help them make the murder look like an accident – details of her travel schedule and constant whereabouts. Meanwhile, "dogdaygod" was also searching the dark web for different ways to launder virtual currency like bitcoin to pay for the assassination.

It was the 35-character bitcoin address that police would eventually find on the smartphone of Stephen Allwine – linking Amy's devoted Christian husband to the assassination plot. But the hit man had been unable to follow through with the kill, and police had discovered something else on Stephen's smartphone.

Apparently, the church elder had some dark secrets. Stephen had spent a few months involved in a relationship with a woman he'd met on Ashley Madison – a website specifically for people looking for extramarital affairs. Michelle, Stephen told police, was from the "western metro Twin Cities" area, and investigators were able to locate her.

"She stated that the two had an intimate relationship for several months during which time they took out-of-town trips together, as well as spent time together locally," the police report read. "She admitted their affair was sexual in nature and provided photographs of the two of them together in which they are hugging and kissing."

This wasn't the first woman Stephen Allwine met on Ashley Madison, however. Police also learned that he had gone on a date with another woman in October 2015, whom he met for dinner at a nearby golf course. The evening ended with a kiss, but they never saw each other again.

Michelle, though, maintained an ongoing relationship with Stephen. She recalled instances when Amy was out of town that Stephen had asked her to come to his home, but that she needed to sneak in the back way to avoid being detected by the home security system. The photographs Michelle shared with authorities were from December 2015, and she said the romance "fizzled" by February – around the same time as "dogdaygod" started investigating the possibility of having Amy Allwine killed by an anonymous hit man from Besa Mafia.

Michelle also told police that if the murder-for-hire plot was true, Stephen Allwine was certainly intelligent enough to pull it off.

According to authorities, the murder scene had been staged to look like a suicide – perhaps an attempt to make it look like Amy had given in to the threats that had been emailed to her from the purported woman named Jane. However, investigators determined that Amy Allwine's death was "inconsistent" with suicide, and charged her husband Stephen with the premeditated murder.

"She's probably dead."

It was Stephen who placed the 911 call on November 13, 2016 – informing the dispatcher that he had arrived home with their nine year old son to find his wife dead in their home. Their son had spotted the body first and brought it to Stephen's attention, which is when he called 911.

When police arrived at approximately 7 p.m., pumpkins were roasting in the kitchen – but Stephen and his son were waiting for police in the open garage. He directed officers to the location of his wife's body, in the bedroom. According to the charging document, Amy was lying on the floor with a pool of blood under her head. Although her body was still warm to the touch, the responding officers were unable to detect a pulse. Later, they would state that Amy was "obviously dead."

Lying near Amy's left forearm and elbow was a gun – a 9mm Springfield XDS. According to Amy's parents, she was right handed.

Additionally, police couldn't find any stippling, or powder burns, on her head, indicating that the gun hadn't been against her head when it went off. There was also no gunpowder, soot, or even blood spatter on Amy's hands.

Investigators discovered traces of Amy's blood elsewhere in the house, though, despite evidence that parts of the home had been cleaned recently. Remnants of bloody footprints were uncovered leading back and forth between the kitchen and the bedroom, and detectives determined that it appeared to be evidence of an "attempted cleanup."

"Agents also found nine separate areas of visible transfer stains and bloodlike substance present on the floor between the master bedroom and laundry room, darkest near the bedroom and progressively lighter near the laundry room," the police document read. "These appeared to be bloody footprints, and were only visible when the crime scene team used luminol and not to the naked eye."

Additional footprints were traced throughout the residence – outside the master bedroom, between the couch and kitchen island, between the dining room table and basement door, in the hallway, in the main floor bathroom, and in the child's bedroom. However, the team noted that "the bloody footprints were not found near any access point to the residence except the garage access door."

Despite the numerous security features that had been added to the house since Cottage Grove police had told the Allwines about the virtual threat on Amy's life, there was no evidence that an outside attacker had killed Stephen's wife. He was the only person coming and going from the property, according to footage captured by the security cameras, and authorities found no signs of forced entry.

Just days after the murder, Stephen Allwine was asked specifically about the blood that appeared to have been cleaned up prior to the arrival of the initial responders. He told detectives that he "had no information about this," adding that no one had been previously injured in the home.

According to Stephen, Amy hadn't been feeling well on the day of her death. She'd mentioned being light-headed, but hadn't wanted to see the doctor about it. According to the Allwines' son, who had been at his grandparents' house when Amy was killed, she was feeling dizzy and his father was going to take her to a clinic.

The last time Stephen saw Amy, he told police, was at around 5:30 p.m., when he left to pick up their son to take him to a gym class. Stephen worked in information technology and had two employers, but worked out of a home office in the basement of the family's home

– a regular shift from 6 a.m. until 5 p.m. from Sunday through Wednesday.

On November 13, detectives learned that Stephen had logged in for work at 6:24 a.m., and remained active until 12:13. He took a lunch break of just more than 41 minutes, and at around 2 p.m., called his in-laws to see if they could pick up their son so that he could get more work done. He said he checked on Amy a couple of times throughout the day, and at around 5 p.m., she said she was fine.

At around 5:30, Stephen left the house to pick up the couple's son from Amy's parents' home. He said he intended to bring the child to a gym class that evening, but while filling his vehicle up with gas, he realized he had forgotten his son's gym shorts at home. Instead of going to the gym, he took his son for dinner at Culver's.

Once they arrived back at the house, the child saw his mother's body in the bedroom and asked Stephen why she was sleeping on the floor. Then, he told police, Stephen replied, "she's probably dead," and called 911.

The home security system that the Allwines had installed in the home was set to record the dates and times that the front and garage doors are opened. On November 13, police learned that after Stephen said he left to pick up his son, no one entered or exited the home until Stephen and the child returned.

"Most notably," the police document stated, "the search warrant return also revealed that after (Amy)'s father left the residence at 2:02 p.m., the service door was opened at 2:40 p.m., 2:42 p.m., and 4:40 p.m."

In the statement he made to police, Stephen claimed that once his son had been picked up by his grandfather, he had been working in the basement until he left at 5:26 p.m. But Stephen's employer reported that after his lunch break on November 13, he did not re-enter the phone queue to finish his shift, and didn't enter any case updates that day – "despite the fact that (Stephen) works on customer issues and is supposed to log all of his activity in his case notes."

Stephen's other employer verified that he didn't log in at all on November 13.

Police noted that Stephen's home office contained "a large amount of computer equipment, which appeared to be very sophisticated and technologically advanced" – however, Stephen had denied having any knowledge about hacking or the dark web in his statement. Instead, he said he knows "how things are supposed to work in the legitimate world."

Investigators quickly learned that Stephen had not been truthful with law enforcement regarding his activity on the internet – information gleaned from examining Stephen's computer revealed that he'd been accessing the dark web since as early as 2014.

Absolute determination

After initially reaching out to Besa Mafia on February 15, the user named "dogdaygod" posted on March 6 that "she" needs "this bitch dead." Amy would be traveling to Moline, Illinois, with a companion, on March 19 and 20 – and according to the post "dogdaygod" made on the website, they didn't care if the companion was killed in the hit, as well. Investigators learned that Amy Allwine had indeed traveled to Moline during that time, when she attended a dog training competition.

However, "dogdaygod" was informed on March 20 that the Besa Mafia hitman had not had the opportunity to kill Amy in Moline – leading the user to suggest that Besa Mafia send someone to complete the hit a few weeks later, when Amy would be in Atlanta. Besa Mafia recommended the use of a sniper for an additional ten bitcoin, or approximately $12,000.

"It was ultimately decided between 'dogdaygod' and Besa Mafia that (Amy) would be killed at her home and the house would be burned afterward," stated police documents. "Besa Mafia stated that with the additional ten bitcoin cost, the plan had a 100 per cent success rate. 'Dogdaygod' agreed to provide the money by the next day."

On March 22, "Dogdaygod" attempted to transfer the bitcoin, and provided Besa Mafia with a specific 34-digit alphanumeric address to be matched with the transfer. According to investigators, these bitcoin addresses are considered unique to each transaction – and during a computer forensics search of Stephen's computer, the specific bitcoin address "dogdaygod" had posted was located on a backed up deleted file – "linking (Stephen) directly to 'dogdaygod.'"

Still, though, Besa Mafia's hitman hadn't completed the job. "Dogdaygod" was informed that their hitman had been caught driving a stolen vehicle and had been taken to jail, but according to local police, "no one was apprehended in Minnesota and western Wisconsin and was arrested in a stolen vehicle and in possession of a gun" during this time. But Besa Mafia didn't stop soliciting money from the user, putting off the hit again and again.

"We have zero information at this point that any of the hits that were ordered on that website were actually carried out," a Minnesota detective told Fox 9 news. "In fact, there is pretty good evidence, I think, that it was just a scam."

In May, Besa Mafia was targeted by an ethical hacker, who published the site's customer list and revealed that the entire operation was a scam. The FBI payed close attention and began investigating the site – while "dogdaygod" had to seek out an alternative solution.

The user popped up on another dark web site looking for a drug dealer in the Minneapolis area – and a forensic search of Stephen Allwine's phone revealed cookies from search engines used to search the dark web were installed on his phone at the same time.

The FBI discovered that "dogdaygod" had been trying to access a drug called scopolamine, or "devil's breath." A derivative of nightshade that can be administered as a powder with no discernable flavour or odor, scopolamine is primarily used to treat nausea. However, the drug is also known to erase a person's memory, according to police documents, and "rendering them incapable of exercising their free will."

While investigating the murder of Amy Allwine, police asked the Ramsey County medical examiner's office to test for the presence of scopolamine – and found that the drug was present in her system, at more than 45 times the concentration of a prescription. Amy had never been prescribed the drug.

"It should be noted that a search of (Amy)'s iPhone 6 revealed that on November 13, 2016, it was last used to search 'Vertigo-Wikipedia' at approximately 2:01 p.m.," police documents stated.

Her time of death was estimated by the medical examiner to have been around 3 p.m. – approximately four hours before police were called. Stephen claimed he'd last seen her and spoken to her more than two hours after the estimated time of death, at around 5:30 p.m. He'd gone into the room to tell Amy that he was leaving to pick up their son, and had found her kneeling by the bed.

"(Stephen) stated that he assumed she was praying, which was not unusual," the police report read. "(Stephen) stated before he left, he asked (Amy) how she was feeling, and she stated she was feeling okay."

"A cold and calculating killer."

Within months, police had gathered enough evidence to link Stephen Allwine to the "dogdaygod" account – and alleged that he had killed his wife after Besa Mafia had failed to complete the ordered hit. Prosecutors claimed he'd been motivated by a mix of religious guilt and piety, as divorce was simply not an option for a church elder who regularly provided marriage counselling.

"He was seeing other women, but he didn't want to divorce (Amy) because of his position in the church," the jury was told by Washington County assistant attorney Jamie Lynn Kreuser.

As members of the United Church of God, the Allwines took a conservative stance on marriage and divorce. According to the church's website, marriage is a "commitment for life" where no "recognized troubles" can justify divorcing a mate "with the freedom to remarry."

"Who would want to do this?" asked Kreuser, noting that as a caring mother, dog owner, and woman of faith, Amy Allwine was not the sort of person who would choose to die by suicide. "Someone who didn't want to be married to her anymore."

The incredible lengths Stephen allegedly went to in order to ensure his wife's death also demonstrated a significant level of sophistication, which was noted by Washington County prosecutor Fred A. Fink Jr. He said Stephen's action "appears to be an absolute determination to kill this woman."

Stephen was also the sole benefactor of his wife's $700,000 life insurance policy, prosecutors said.

But the defense argued that there was insufficient physical evidence connecting Stephen with the crime – all forensics had been able to find was a "particle characteristic of gunshot residue" on Stephen's right hand from the sample he'd given to police after Amy's death.

According to Stephen's attorney, Kevin DeVore, prosecutors had built a case on "theories with gaps," and incorporated plenty of speculation to "bridge those gaps."

"It sounds like an amazing story – but it's not a TV show or a movie, but real life," he said. "Just because he had an affair doesn't mean he killed his wife or even didn't love his wife."

The jury disagreed with the defense's argument, despite Fink's own admission that the case was "entirely circumstantial." On January 31, 2018, after just eight hours of deliberation, they found Stephen Allwine guilty of first-degree murder for the premeditated attack on his wife.

Addressing the courtroom at his sentencing just days later, Stephen stated that he had always loved his wife and did not kill her – adding, "I've never asked for anything except to work for God."

"I never went to sleep, and I never woke up without kissing her," he said. "The grief of losing her is tremendous."

He also claimed that the couple had never even argued, noting that "no one ever talked bad about our relationship." During his statement, he insinuated that an unknown assailant had entered the house through a patio door which had been left unlocked.

"Even though she's gone, she's gone knowing I loved her," Stephen said. "The only image I have in my mind is one of my smiling, beautiful wife."

Judge B. William Ekstrum was unable to conceal his irritation, and told Stephen, "you are an incredible actor, a hypocrite, and a cold and calculating killer."

"We're looking at a complete narcissist," Fink added after the sentencing. "His elocution was all about him – not Amy or her death."

"The most complex case."

Ekstrum sentenced Stephen to life in prison with no possibility of parole – the mandatory sentence for a conviction of first degree murder. His term is to be served at St. Cloud Prison. Stephen said that during his time at the Washington County Jail, he's met drug addicts, child molesters, and kidnappers – and had been conducting regular bible study sessions.

"I'm going to take my bible to St. Cloud (Prison)," Stephen said, "and see what happens."

He no longer serves as a church elder, however, as the Council of Elders at the United Church of God removed Stephen from ministry after he was initially charged with Amy's murder in 2017. While the church did release a brief statement following the sentencing, it offered no "speculative comments" regarding the verdict.

"It is our fervent hope that all will continue praying to our merciful Father about the entire situation and be compassionate about what the extended families are going through," the statement read. "We can have confidence that our all-knowing God is aware of all aspects regarding this tragic situation."

Prosecutors were pleased with the result, although Fink noted making the conviction required the jury to almost piece together a "jigsaw puzzle" of evidence.

"We believe the jury did the right thing," he said after the sentence was handed down. "They had a lot of pieces of evidence to go through ... I've been doing this 43 years and it's probably the most complex case I've ever tried. It's fair that this defendant spends the rest of his life in prison."

It was also one of the more complex investigations ever undertaken by Cottage Grove police, according to detective Sgt. Randy McAlister. As many as five detectives worked the case over two months – with the first month requiring them to set aside much of the rest of their workload to focus on the investigation full-time.

"I think the big difference between this and a more common murder the dark web, the internet connection – that's what's really been taking a lot of time," he said. "This is the first case involving death threats on a purported dark web website that we've ever dealt with. This is definitely the most in-depth."

Kreuser said that throughout the sensationalized trial, prosecutors stayed focused on the victim and her loved ones – despite significant media attention.

"At the end of the day, justice was served," she said, "and I'm glad for Amy and her family."

Many of Amy's family and friends provided victim impact statements during the six day trial – though few of these accounts were critical of Stephen. The courtroom was filled with people who knew the couple, either through Amy's business or the family's dedication to the church.

"It was very supportive for the entire thing," said DeVore. "It goes beyond the love one might expect."

Still, Amy's parents were stung by Stephen's betrayal, and called him a "selfish person." They added they'd been "astonished" to hear how Stephen had spent months plotting their daughter's murder – at Amy's wedding twenty years earlier, her father remembered how he "put her hand into Steve's and asked him to take good care of my little girl."

Amy's sister, Julie Brown, told the court about how Amy had "lived in fear every waking moment of the last months of her life," thanks to the anonymous death threats she'd received, and the murder-for-hire plot the FBI had warned her about. Even simple tasks like going grocery shopping "spurred intense anxiety" for Amy.

"We've lost so much," Brown said, "but with God's grace, all is not lost."

After the verdict, Amy's parents and siblings released another statement.

"We can summon no words to describe life without Amy," it read. "We loved her and miss her tremendously. We now turn to the path ahead of privately healing and grieving."

THE VALENTINES DAY MURDER

ANA BENSON

Richard and Stacy Schoeck had a perfect marriage, or at least it looked ideal for their friends and family. Even though they have been together for a long time, they seemed to have eyes only for each other. Richard was Stacy's fifth husband and everyone was certain that he was indeed the love of her life. The couple still went on dates and celebrated their love in every way possible. So when Valentine's Day in 2010 came around, the Schoecks were setting up a romantic little getaway and a card exchange in a picturesque Belton Bridge Park which is located in Lula, Georgia.

Lula is a quiet little tourist town so when their Police Department received a frantic phone call with Stacy on the other end of the line, they knew something serious had happened. The town was shocked to discover that a murder occurred right there in their calm little oasis. But soon enough, the sinister plot started to unravel and the law enforcement realized that things were not as they seemed.

So what made Stacy Schoeck turn on her loving husband and who helped her with the murderous plan?

Early life

Stacy Morgan was born in 1971 in Florida. Her childhood wasn't perfect at all and her father died when she was really young. This left a permanent mark on Stacy even though her mother remarried soon and she did have a father figure in her life. She was also molested during this time frame by an individual who remained anonymous to everyone around her. Stacy grew up to be a lovely teenage girl who would fall in love easily. She met her first husband while she was still in high school and the couple got married shortly after. Unfortunately, he wasn't what Stacy was looking for and it took her two years to come to this conclusion. She filed for a divorce and the two separated.

When Stacy was twenty years old, she met her second husband. Soon after the wedding, Stacy found out that she was pregnant with her first child. The marriage lasted a little more than a year and she once again filed for a divorce when her son was just a toddler. Instead of being beaten down by two failed marriages, Stacy remained strong and made a decision to improve herself. After all, she was only twenty-two years old. She applied for college and got accepted. Stacy moved on to raise her son on her own and earn a degree in psychology and nursing at the same time.

She managed to find the employment as soon as she got out of college. Stacy was still very optimistic about her love life and wanted to find someone to spend the rest of her life with. She met her third husband in 1997 but unfortunately, the marriage was short-lived once again. It lasted for only six weeks. Stacy decided to date casually in the future and gave birth to her second son in 1998. She was still a single mother but this didn't seem to bother her at all.

Stacy did need to improve her financial status and she found a better job opportunity at a clinic which was located in Atlanta. The family moved over there and she was ready to start over. She got an excellent position at the hospital's administration with the possibility of even better promotion. She would assist the doctors on a daily basis with various tasks. Stacy was a successful and independent woman who was capable of taking care of her two small boys on her own.

But something was still missing and Stacy was longing for a partner who would be there for her. She was tired of casual encounters and needed some stability. So in 2001 she married for the fourth time and moved out to a small town near Atlanta. She got pregnant once again and gave birth to her third son. She lived in a large house with her fourth husband and it seemed that her life was absolutely perfect. Her boys were happy and they loved the suburban lifestyle. On the other hand, Stacy was still unhappy. Soon after the separation from her fourth husband in 2005, Stacy met Richard Schoeck, a graphic designer who was slightly older than her. He was a patient at the hospital where Stacy worked at the time. The two hit it off immediately.

Richard Schoeck was an adventurer who lived his life to the maximum. Stacy was immediately attracted to his positive attitude and passionate outlook. Richard accepted Stacy's sons like they were his own and would often organize family outings that included the entire family. She loved how different Richard was from all of her previous husbands and thought that she had finally found the one.

Unconcerned about Stacy's previous failed marriages, Richard still wanted to make their relationship permanent. The couple did get married in 2007 but the ceremony wasn't standard at all. Stacy and Richard eloped and told everyone about the wedding once they came back home. It was in Richard's nature to do something so spontaneous and Stacy adored him for that.

Richard became a stay at home dad after the wedding and he would form a close bond with Stacy's boys. He was very involved with their school and hobbies so he ended up adopting the youngest two. He really did accept this small family as his own and wanted the best for the boys. Everyone approved of Richard and Stacy's family hoped that she finally found the man of her life. Unfortunately, this marriage would end up tragically in just a couple of years.

The murder of Richard Schoeck

Prior to Valentine's Day in February of 2010, Stacy invited Richard on a small romantic getaway to the town of Lulu, Georgia. They were supposed to meet in Belton Bridge Park which is a secluded area near the town itself and exchange gifts there. This wasn't unusual for the Schoecks because they would often go on different adventures that were supposed to spice up their love life. The Police dispatchers received a frantic phone call sometime after the nightfall. Stacy was screaming that her husband was shot and robbed. He wasn't showing any signs of life.

The police arrived at the scene of the crime and sure enough, Richard's body was lying next to his pickup truck. The blood was both inside and outside of the vehicle which meant that several shots were fired. At least one bullet hit him while he was still in the driver's seat or getting out of the car. He crawled out, perhaps to run away or defend himself. The shooter continued firing the gun until they were certain that Richard was dead.

The investigators immediately closed off the area and examined the tire tracks which were visible in the surrounding mud. They noticed that the third vehicle was definitely there and that it left the scene of the crime prior to the arrival of Stacy. The law enforcement marked them as the evidence. However, there were some red flags that indicated that this wasn't a standard robbery. For instance, Richard's valet was still in the car and his jewelry was on him. Nothing was taken from the scene.

Stacy wasn't a suspect at the time but the police escorted her to the station in order to interview her and get as many details as possible. Lulu is a quiet town where crime rarely happens so the law enforcement couldn't zero in on any possible reason why Richard was shot. One theory suggested that he might have interrupted another couple at Belton Bridge Park because it was a common meeting ground for lovebirds who wanted to spend some time together outside of their homes.

The interviews and investigation

Once Stacy got to the station, she started talking. She was asked to explain what they were doing at the remote park and she admitted that they did have problems in their marriage. She thought this would be the perfect time to add some flare to their relationship. Since Richard was a stay at home dad and she had difficult work hours, the two simply couldn't get any alone time to spend with each other. She was becoming desperate and unhappy.

She quickly admitted to having an affair to the shock of everyone who was present in the interrogation room. Her lover was a fellow co-worker from the hospital who was significantly younger than Richard. His name was Juan and he was a complete opposite of Stacy's husband. She needed intimacy and she fell in love with someone else who could give her everything she craved for. Stacy even took her lover to Las Vegas just a couple of weeks prior to the murder of her husband.

The detectives were interested in the affair and started asking questions related to the possibility that Stacy wanted to get out of her marriage with Richard in order to be with her new man. Stacy told them that she did think about leaving Richard but that no particular plans were made. She knew how much her children loved him and getting a divorce would probably break their hearts. They focused on Stacy's lover but she quickly debunked their claims by saying that he is not violent at all and that she cannot imagine him being involved with anything involving guns or shooting.

But Stacy did say that Juan knew about the rendezvous in the park so the police decided to call him up for an interview the next morning. Juan seemed oblivious to the events that took place last night and he told the detectives that Stacy claimed her relationship with Richard was open. This meant that each of them had someone on the side. Juan didn't seem to be bothered by this arrangement at all so the investigators started doubting their possible theory. Plus, Juan had a solid alibi for the time of the murder because he was in another city.

They were left without any solid lead in this case so it was time to look a bit further and include as much aid as possible. The park is a fairly isolated place but there was a nearby cell phone tower that covered the entire area. The investigators knew that if a call was placed from that location on the night of the murder, they would have the number listed. And it turned out that this was a crucial move made by the investigators because it would lead them in the right direction.

The list of calls was short because that cell tower is not in an urban area. The detectives used the contact information which was stored in both Stacy's and Richard's phones and they tried to find the match. Stacy's phone had the number that was called sometime around the murder. The contact info itself stood out because it said Mr. Results. The investigators were slightly confused because they had no idea who this person was. But calling him up would probably shed some light on the events that occurred on Valentine's Day.

The police quickly identified the mystery man who was present at the scene of the crime that night. His name was Reginald Coleman and he worked as a private fitness instructor in Atlanta. Coleman was born in Philadelphia but his criminal past led him to move out from his hometown and try to start over in another state. He was incarcerated in the past but managed to clean up his act. Coleman was doing fine financially and owned a fairly popular gym. As far as the local police force knew, he was staying away from any type of crime.

Todd Woodten who would become Coleman's attorney during the trial said the following on his client: "Reginald was a true survivor. He was street-savvy and always had a hustle going on. He did a lot of things for youth, trying to keep them off the street and keep them safe."

Once the police managed to attain the call records from Reginald Coleman's cell phone, they found the number he had called from the Belton Bridge Park. The investigators thought they would see Stacy Schoeck's digits but they were surprised with their discovery. Coleman called another woman - Lynitra Ross. The detectives then realized that the whole plot was more complicated that they initially assumed and that there are more players involved with the murder of Richard Schoeck. So how did all of them fit together?

After speaking to Coleman's friends, the police found out that Lynitra Ross was his ex-girlfriend who would often resurface in his life. But there was another detail that connected Lynitra to the murder – she worked at the same hospital as Stacy Schoeck and two of them were really good friends. Stacy was Lynitra's boss and a landlord. Since there was a third set of tire marks on the scene of the murder, the detectives quickly determined that the model did not fit the tires on Reginald's car. This did sidetrack them a bit but they were still determined to find out what really happened.

The investigators were certain that they did, in fact, have their suspect and that was Stacy Schoeck. However, they still had to connect the dots so they dug even further into the phone records of those three. There was a message exchange on the night prior to the murder of Richard Schoeck between the three parties. However, the most interesting clue was Stacy's bank account which clearly stated that she sent a total of $10,000 to Lynitra's account which she passed along to Reginald.

The arrests

Since the topic of the third vehicle was still the big unknown, the police started going through all cars which were somehow related to Stacy, Lynitra, and Reginald. And soon enough they were onto something. Stacy did have one car which she sold soon after the murder. It wasn't registered to her but she did use it often in order to drive her relatives or get them groceries. They were surprised to find out that Stacy put their vehicle on the market but she told them that they will get a newer model as a gift from her.

The police became very suspicious of this story so they tracked down the new owner and took a look at the tires as well as the insides of the car. And yes, the tire marks matched perfectly. Stacy Schoeck borrowed that car to Reginald Coleman on that fatal Valentine's Day. The evidence against Coleman was piling up and he was arrested on May 25th, 2010. But as soon as the interrogation started, he denied any involvement with Stacy Schoeck or the murder of her husband.

Lynitra Ross was arrested a couple of hours after Reginald but she also refused to provide the investigators with any useful information. It was time to pick up Stacy as well so the police arrived at the medical center she worked at and led her straight to the station. The investigators had plenty of circumstantial evidence to accuse her of the murder and they didn't have to wait for her accomplices to start talking about the crime. All three of them were in custody and it was time to face the justice for their actions.

Psychological assessment

Stacy Schoeck was put through a psychological assessment prior to the trial itself in order to determine if she had any underlying problems which were unknown to her or her family. The murder was well planned so she clearly wasn't distraught at the time which meant that Stacy knew exactly what she was doing when she asked her friend Lynitra to help her get rid of her husband.

The psychologists took a closer look at her prior relationships and marriages which ended in divorce. The reason for her unhappiness might lay in the fact that she lost her biological father when she was young and she was unable to connect to anyone. Not to forget that Stacy was also molested when she was just a child.

It was obvious that Stacy Schoeck was manipulative and knew how to get exactly what she wanted in every situation. Her intelligence was obviously high because she did put herself through school and successfully earned her degrees. However, her actions towards Richard Schoeck show that Stacy was also a sociopath because she hired a man to murder her husband and continued to live her life as nothing happened.

She mourned her husband publicly and got very emotional in front of her friends and family every time they saw her. The fact that she selected Valentine's Day as the date of the execution speaks volumes about her cold-heartedness towards Richard Schoeck.

The trials of Ross and Coleman

The first of three to stand a trial was Lynitra Ross. She entered the courtroom in May 2012 and was facing charges for a murder. After all, she was a co-conspirator who helped Stacy Schoeck find the hitman who would eventually pull the trigger and take Richard's life. Stacy was also present in the courtroom but she wasn't the accused in this situation. As a matter of fact, she testified on the side of the prosecution.

Stacy Schoeck was cooperating with the law enforcement and made a deal regarding her sentencing. She did everything to avoid the death penalty and was ready to talk about the murder of her husband. It was clear that her deeds were out in the open and she said the following as she took the stand: "I'm going to testify truthfully for Richard. It's all I can give his mom and his family and the children — all I can give them is the truth."

The jury then heard the story about the murder plot. Stacy Schoeck had the idea to take her husband's life in December 2009 after she noticed that her boys were acting strangely. They were getting into troubles and she started to suspect that they might be victims of molestation. She remembered how she behaved during the time she was assaulted as a child and found the connection. Of course, her first suspect was Richard because he was always with the boys.

Stacy also said: "I was just so fixated in my mind that Richard was doing something wrong that I said, 'I don't want the cops, I don't want a divorce, I want him dead.'" She then admitted to asking an unnamed man to help her kill her husband but he stopped returning her calls. Then she talked to her friend and co-worker Lynitra Ross and told her about her suspicions. Lynitra responded with the suggestion that they talk to her ex-boyfriend who would know what to do because he was "an experienced hitman".

After Lynitra Ross contacted Coleman, the two woman drove to his house and sat down with him in order to agree on some finer details regarding the hit. They talked and ate food from Zaxby's. Stacy suggested the park as the perfect place for executing her husband because he wouldn't suspect a thing. Reginald and Stacy agreed on the amount of money she would pay him for the murder, as well as on the vehicle he would take to the park. All three of them went to Belton Bridge Park so that Stacy could show him the exact place where her husband will be waiting.

Stacy noted in her testimony the following: "The only times I ever saw or spoke to Reginald Coleman was the day we had Zaxby's that afternoon and the following Saturday when we went up to Belton

Bridge. Everything else was done through Lynitra." She also added that she had given Lynitra the property she was renting to her as the payment for the help.

Lynitra's defense lawyers took the stand and told the jury that Stacy's testimony which involved the molestation claims was slightly off due to the fact that she admitted to having an affair in the first interview she gave after the murder. She didn't mention anything related to the possible sexual abuse of her children.

In August of 2012, Lynitra Ross was sentenced to life in prison. There would be no possibility of a parole either. Even though she didn't pull the trigger, she was the person who set up Stacy and Reginald to meet. Therefore, she was directly involved in the murder plot.

It was later determined that Richard Schoeck didn't have anything to do with child molestation but Stacy's plan was already completed and her husband was dead. The investigators took her claims seriously and talked to the middle boy who immediately said that he never accused Richard of anything. As a matter of fact, he never even talked to his mother about the alleged abuse. However, this didn't stop Stacy's attorneys from building their case around this.

Reginald Coleman's trial didn't last long because as soon as he appeared in front of the judge in November of 2012, he pleaded guilty to the murder of Richard Schoeck. He also faced charges for owning the firearm as a convicted felon. Stacy Schoeck was set to testify against him as well, which meant providing the courtroom with the full account of Reginald's actions.

Reginald Coleman agreed to kill Richard Schoeck after he heard the story of the alleged molestation directly from Stacy and Lynitra. Since he grew up in foster care, he often listened to the stories from his friends about their own abuse. Coleman thought that he could help the boys have a normal childhood by eliminating the threat from their life. He pleaded guilty in order to avoid the death penalty which was already on the table if he went on a trial. Coleman received the punishment of life in prison without the possibility of a parole and some additional years for the possession of the firearm.

Stacy Schoeck's trial

Once Ross and Coleman received their sentences, it was time for Stacy to appear in court for her own trial. The proceedings began in December of 2012 at Hall County Courtroom. Since Stacy cooperated with the prosecution in the trials of Coleman and Ross, the death penalty was off the table. Judge Jason Deal listened to the witnesses who described Richard Schoeck as a loving father and an exceptional friend who would never harm anyone. Stacy's defense attorneys once again repeated the story of the alleged abuse and claimed that her actions were severe because she wanted to protect her children from the aggressor.

When Stacy took the stand, she admitted to the crime and asked the judge to give her mercy. The defense told the courtroom about Stacy's own abuse and that she was acting erratically. However, the fact that the murder was planned months before it happened painted a picture of someone who wanted to eliminate her husband. Stacy had plenty of time to make sure that Richard was really the abuser and contact the law enforcement but she failed to do so.

Stacy's lawyers asked Judge Deal to consider giving Stacy a possibility of a parole and to keep in mind her troubled past. They also pointed out that Stacy was behaving well in prison and that she deserves a second chance. However, she received the punishment of life in prison without a chance to get out after serving thirty years which was the primary goal of her defense team.

Attorney Lee Darragh who led the prosecution said: "Judge Jason Deal appropriately recognized that Stacey Schoeck was the engine that put this train in motion, until the death of her husband. Without her involvement, this would not have occurred." The courtroom was filled with emotions because a large number of Richard's friends showed up for the hearing. One of the saddest moments was when Stacy's mother read a note which was written by her youngest boy which said: "I miss her every hour of every day, just like Daddy Richard."

Initially, Stacy Schoeck and Lynitra Ross were placed in two separate prisons in order to avoid any possible conflicts between the two but they were soon moved to the same facility – Pulaski State Prison. Stacy's family was left to wonder what was really the reason for this heinous crime because the exact motive was never uncovered. They got the custody of Stacy's three sons.

THE MURDER OF ASHLEY FALLIS

SARAH THOMPSON-CARLOS

42

What reason would a perfectly happy and healthy 28-year-old mother of two have for taking her own life? That is the question that seems to perpetually surround the case of Ashley Fallis, who was found dead of a bullet wound in the early morning hours of New Year's day in 2012. A beautiful young woman, Ashley was small and slight, with a bright smile and an attractive face. A photo of herself on her wedding days shows her kneeling it the grass with her children: her two daughters, Madelynn and Jolie, and her son, Blake. Her blond hair is elegantly pinned back off her face, and there's such joy on her face. It's hard to imagine that this young woman, so vibrantly fully of life, would take her own life and leave behind her three children, all under the age of 10 at the time of her death.

According to statistics gathered by the CDC, over half of American women who are killed have relations to intimate partner violence. After analyzing the murders of women in 18 different states, spanning across the years of 2003 to 2014, the CDC focused on exactly 10,018 different female deaths. Of all of those deaths, 55% of of them were related to intimate partner violence. Intimate partner violence can be described as family members, lovers, boyfriends, partners and spouses. That that definition in mind, even more chilling was the finding that in 93% of those cases, the perpetrator was a romantic partner, either current or former. It becomes even more unnerving to find out that 54% of those deaths were gun deaths.

It draws the question, with a statistical trend like this, is it possible that an otherwise happy woman, with her husband and children, would take her own life? Despite what her friends and family knew about her, was it possible that Ashley Fallis was hiding a secret depression so deep that she took a gun to herself to end it all?

Most people can't say that they married their high school sweetheart, but Ashley was one of the lucky few who could. Unfortunately, that relationship didn't last. They married soon after their high school graduation, and had two daughters: Madelynn and

Jolie. Despite the children, the marriage crumbled and fell apart, and the two divorced. It was in 2007 that Ashley met Tom Fallis, who would surely change her life. Tom Fallis was a responsible man, and he seemed to have his life together.

It was only one month into their new, budding relationship that Ashley fell pregnant once again. That was how Blake was brought into the family. Their son was what brought Ashley and Tom together, despite the shortness of their new relationship. It was only two weeks after Blake was born that Ashley and Tom decided to make their family official. Tom adopted Madelynn and Jolie, and they couple married.

As beautiful a story as it seems, Ashley's family felt as if the whole thing was moving quite quickly. After all, Ashley and Tom had only known one another for a month before she fell pregnant. Perhaps their relationship had grown closer throughout her pregnancy, and then after the birth of their son. Still, it was mostly unknown to Jenna Fox, Ashley's mother, and Joel Raguindin, Ashley's adoptive father. Ashley and her mother were extremely close, much more like friends than mother and daughter. Raguindin explained how they had tried to talk Ashley out of it before the wedding.

Tom Fallis seemed like an alright guy, at first. After all, he was ready to start a family. He seemed to have his life together. But, slowly, Ashley's family began to notice that there was something wrong with him. Tom Fallis had a problem with needing to be right all the time. He was aggressive, and seemed to always be ready to argue. Jenna Fox noticed it, and she didn't like it. Ashley's family was worried by the way Tom was acting, but there seemed to be nothing to draw the couple away from one another.

After the wedding, Ashley and Tom decided to settle down together with their three children in the small town of Evans, Colorado, just an hour outside of Denver. Tom took a jobs as a corrections officers at the Weld County Sheriff's Office, stationed at a local prison. Meanwhile, Ashley began working as a respiratory therapist. Those who knew Tom Fallis thought that he took the job as a corrections officer to feed his ego. After all, he was an aggressive person, according to Jenna Fox. He was also insecure. "He wanted total control of her," Jenna Fox told 48 Hours.

Jenna Fox also felt that she was a threat to Tom. After all, she was one of the only people that he could not isolate Ashley away from. The bond before mother and daughter was, seemingly, stronger than the bond between new husband and wife. The pressure to keep a balance between her new family with Tom and her relationship with her parents was put on Ashley. That pressure only increased when Blake, only just a toddler, was diagnosed with a brain condition. The condition was chronic, and would start to require almost all of Ashley's attention. Ashley was a doting mother, and did all that she could to give her son the attention and help that he required.

The constant attention that her son required, paired with the stress of Tom's increasingly controlling behavior was starting to take it's toll. Ashley was quite anxious, and overwhelmed with the situation as a whole. Still, Fox and Raguindin had never once suspected that Ashley was particularly depressed, nor did they suspect that she was suicidal. It just didn't seem like their daughter.

Still, Ashley and Tom's marriage was starting to feel the weight of that pressure. The two were considering a divorce, but apparently their relationship was slowly getting better as the holidays approached. The couple were planning a New Year's Eve party. And beyond that, they had received happy news. As the holidays closed in, Ashley had thought that she'd become pregnant again. They suspected that their family was about to grow even more.

That happiness only lasted so long. After she had gotten that positive pregnancy test, Ashley had stopped taking any medication just in case. After all, false positives happened all the time, and she wanted to make sure that whether the pregnancy was legitimate before she continued on. However, the day of their New Year's Eve party came and

Ashley began to bleed. Perhaps she had simply not been pregnant at all, or perhaps she was miscarrying. Whatever the cause of her bleeding, Ashley had been excited for the new baby. Learning that she was no longer pregnant caused her some significant sadness.

Despite learning that she wouldn't be a new mother once more, Ashley and Tom went forward with their New Year's Eve party all the same. After all, the invitations had been made, and the guests were on their way.

The part was a disaster. Jenna Fox describes the way that the tension between herself and her daughter's husband was becoming almost unbearable. Fox told 48 Hours that she "knew that Tom hated me". Despite the friction between mother-in-law and husband, the party was beginning to wind down without major incident - that is, until Tom Fallis went into a blinding rage because he had overheard Ashley's uncle offering her some marijuana. He began to swear, furious and loud. He told her that she didn't need to get high, even if she was still upset about the miscarriage. He told her, "It happened," and then told her that they were leaving, and to "Fuck everybody," and just let it go.

As Ashley's parents were leaving the party, they observed as Tom went into the bedroom, slamming the door behind him. Ashley walked them out, and they said their goodbyes at 12:04 am, after the New Year's ball had already dropped. Fox didn't observe anything out of the ordinary about her daughter. She didn't seem upset by Tom's behavior, after all. It wasn't out of place for Tom to act like this, and become enraged and swear. As Fox and Raguindin hugged their daughter and said their goodbyes on the front porch, they had no idea that this would be the last time that they saw their daughter alive.

Ashley isn't here any longer to tell us the rest of her story. What we know of that night is what Tom Fallis claims happened, and the autopsy reports, and the police records. As they guests filtered out of the house, they were among the last to see Ashley Fallis alive. When the last guest left and the door closed, no one but Ashley and Tom Fallis really know what happened that night that lead to the death of Ashley early in the hours of New Year's Day.

According to Tom Fallis, Ashley came into the bedroom in a defiant mood, and he said that she told him that if she wanted to get high, then she would get high. Tom told police that he told her to do whatever she wanted. Tom told the police that he had been in their closet, getting changed, when he heard the sound of her loading a gun across the room. Supposedly, it was the .9mm Taurus that Ashley kept under her mattress. As Tom walked out of the closet, he asked her what she was doing - and then, he heard the sound of a gunshot. Tom claims that he ran across the room to where Ashley was and held her head where the gunshot wound was, then grabbed the phone and dialed 911.

A recording of Tom Fallis' panicked 911 call plays Tom's voice, panicked and screaming: "My wife just shot herself in the head! Please help me! Please help me!" While the 911 operator tries to get his exact location and calm him down, Tom's voice comes through the call, tinny and screaming: "Ashley, no! Ashley, no!"

Finally, as the 911 operator tries to get more information, Tom can be heard shouting at his dying wife: "You are not leaving me! You are not leaving me! Stay right here!"

All in all, Ashley's family had only been gone for ten minutes. Ten minutes previous, Ashley had been on the porch, saying goodbye to all of her loved ones after celebrating the incoming of the new year. Her parents weren't even home, yet. They were still on the road when they saw the squad cars that were dispatched due to the call made by Tom.

At the hospital, Jenna Fox told 48 Hours that she knew, from the moment that she had seen her daughter lying in the hospital bed, that Tom Fallis had been involved. Perhaps it was a mother's intuition. Whatever the reason, Fox had no doubt that her daughter wouldn't have committed suicide. Even with the grief of her miscarriage hanging heavy over her that New Year's Eve, she was surrounded by her family and loved ones. Fox didn't believe for one second that suicide was an option for her daughter.

Ashley Fallis hadn't died immediately from that gunshot wound. She arrived at the hospital with severe trauma to the brain. But she wouldn't recover. The last time that her parents saw her alive and sentient was on the porch, ten minutes before she took a gunshot wound to the head.

But what happened? Tom's versions of events are clear. Ashley came into the bedroom, angry, and took a gun to her own head. Despite the fact that statistics put female suicides by firearm at only 31.2% (compared to male suicide by firearm at 56.4%), is it possible that Ashley had chosen such method? Women who commit suicide are often going to chose a less painful method, and one that would not leave behind such a mess. Pills and cutting of the wrists are much more popular methods when it comes to women who take their own life. But perhaps it was Ashley's grief that had driven her to take her own life with the gun she kept under her mattress.

Was it?

Despite the fact that Tom Fallis called in a suicide to 911, the police thought that it was important to question him about what happened. The police brought Tom Fallis into the station early on the morning of New Year's day, leaving his parents to watch his and Ashley's three small children. While Tom's frantic 911 call had seemed genuine, the police weren't all too sure. Neighbors had reported that they could hearing yelling and arguing coming from the couples house. Being questioned by Detective Rita Wolf, Tom was immediately put under scrutiny. The wound on Ashley's head was near the back. When told that her wound wasn't consistent with a suicide shot, Tom simply replied, "Bullshit! I didn't shoot my wife."

When investigators searched Tom's body, they found scratches on his chest, which he had said were from himself itching at his newly shaved chest. But that's not all investigators found. When they went into the Fallis' residence to take stock of the scene of the suicide, they discovered something strange. Tom's version of events had Ashley coming into the bedroom in an agitated state, then simply going across the room to retrieve her gun from under her mattress and shoot herself in the head. The state of the house, however, was inconsistent with that story.

Investigators found that pictures had been strewn from their place on the wall. It looked as if there had been a struggle. Not only that, but divorce papers had been found placed in a drawer. Tom Fallis had insisted that things had been going alright with him and Ashley, and that while they had been struggling before, things were moving in the right direction. The mere presence of divorce papers seemed to speak volumes, going against what Tom Fallis claimed was going on in his supposedly happy family.

At the hospital, Ashley Fallis had bruises on her legs. All of the evidence that investigators were digging up seemed to show that something else had gone down after all the guests had left the party - and that it wasn't suicide. Still, even after Tom Fallis was questioned for hours, he was released later that morning without charges being pressed against him.

Raguindin told 48 Hours that he and Fox were "shocked that they let him go." Even more shocking was what happened after that. Detective Wolf had told Tom Fallis that she didn't believe that Ashley could have inflicted that gunshot wound on herself. The position of the wound at the back of her head wasn't consistent with a suicide. Still, on January 5th, the coroner made an official ruling, and Ashley's death was listed as a suicide. Officially, the case was closed.

That seemed to be that. Ashley Fallis, wife, mother of three and devoted caretaker of her special needs son, was said to have taken her own life in the early morning hours of January 1st, ten minutes after waving goodbye to her family on the front porch after their New Year's Eve party.

The story for Tom Fallis, however, would go on. He packed up his children and moved them to Indiana, where he would attend graduate school. Despite the stress and strain of the relationship between Tom and Ashley's parents, they were determined to keep in contact with him for the sake of continuing a relationship with their grandchildren. After all, they were the only pieces of their daughter that they had left.

Life went on. For two years, Ashley's parents mourned their daughter's untimely death, and maintained a relationship with a man that they hated for the sake of their grandchildren. It seemed like no one else believed that Ashley wouldn't have taken her own life, and no one else believed that Tom Fallis was at fault. Until, one day, two years after Ashley's death, a man named Justin Joseph caught wind of the case. Joseph was a television news reporter with a source in law enforcement. Turns out, Ashley's parents weren't the only ones who were perturbed by the case.

Two years had passed, but Joseph took on investigating Ashley's story, anyway. Nothing seemed to sit right, and it was finally time to bring Ashley the justice that she deserved. Months were put into interviewing neighbors and friends who had already been cleared by the police, all of their statements taken and their concerns brushed off. In April of 2014, Joseph interviewed one of the Fallis' next door neighbors, Nick Glover, and found just what he needed to bust the case of Ashley's death wide open again.

Glover's versions of events differed from Tom Fallis'. According to Glover, he had heard Tom come out of the house, so he knelt down beneath the window sill to stay out of sight while he listened. Tom's parents were outside, and Glover could hear Tom saying, "Oh my god, I can't believe I did it." When his parents pressed him for more information, Glover heard Tom say: "I shot her." Of course, this wasn't the first time that Glover had told someone what had happened. In fact, the day that he was questioned by Evans Police, Glover told exactly the same thing to a Detective Michael Yates.

Glover's mother, Kathy Glover, had gotten a phone call that night from another neighbor by the name of Chelsey Arrigo. She told them to call the police, because she was sure that Tom Fallis had just shot his wife. Arrigo had heard Ashley yelling for Tom to get off of her, and the pop of the gun.

Everyone seemed to know what happened that night, and nothing was done. In fact, Detective Yates hadn't even written the report correctly. In his report of the incident that night, he quoted Arrigo as saying Ashley shot herself, not that Tom Fallis had shot her. Yates had also claimed that Glover had never told him about overhearing Tom admit to the murder of his wife. With contradicting statements, no one knew why a follow-up hadn't been given. Arrigo hadn't even been interviewed, despite knowing that Kathy had been in contact with her the night of Ashley's death. The case had been handled poorly from open to close, and no one seemed to know why.

Joseph found another person who had heard Tom Fallis admit the the murder of his wife: a sheriff's deputy who happened to be at the scene. It wasn't until two years later that he came forward to tell the investigators what he head heard. It's unclear as to why the case of Ashley Fallis wasn't treated as a homicide, or why no one seemed to take Glover seriously when he had told them what he heard, or why the sheriff's deputy said nothing to anyone until two years after the fact.

Was it a cover-up by the police? Or was it simply serious human error that caused the police not to go back and re-interview the people who had said they heard Tom Fallis admitting to murder? It seems hard to believe that the police would simply brush away Detective Wolf pointing out the position of the gunshot wound on Ashley's head, and two witnesses who had heard Tom Fallis saying clearly, "I shot her." One would want to hope that it was a serious error, and not the police deliberately looking the other way. There's no explanation for why Ashley Fallis' death was ruled a suicide, despite the evidence of a struggle in their house, and the witnesses that described Tom Fallis has raging and angry that night.

Whatever the reason that Ashley's case was closed, it was Justin Joseph that got it re-opened. His investigating opened up some serious questions about that night, and why the police had moved forward to rule her death a suicide. The case was reopened by a Evans, Colorado neighbor, Fort Collins, along with their much larger police force.

Tom Fallis had more information for the police, too. Two years after Ashley's death, Tom Fallis came forward during the new investigation with a suicide note that Ashley had supposedly written. There were several notes, one which read: "Dear Tom [...] I'm sorry for your pain. [...] I am a failure at everything." Of course, the timing of the suicide notes were suspicious. If Ashley had committed suicide, wouldn't the notes have shown up that first night?

Finally, it seemed like justice for Ashley Fallis was going to happen. In November of 2014, a grand jury made the decision to indict Tom Fallis for the murder of his wife. He was arrested in Indiana, and his children were put under the care of his parents. Tom Fallis had gotten away with putting his wife's supposed suicide in the past for almost three years. It wasn't until March of 2016 that Tom was finally put on trial.

The defense used Ashley's history of mental illness, anxiety, and the pain of her miscarriage to build a case against a dead woman. They claimed that it was Ashley who had shot herself in the middle of a crisis that early morning on New Year's Day. They pointed out that Ashley had been drinking at the party, and that there was even a history of suicide in her family: her uncle's mother and brother both died from suicide by gunshot. Was this just another suicide in a long line of tragedies? The defense seemed to think so.

Still, when Ashley's therapist took the stand, he made it clear that he did not consider Ashley a danger to herself or others. Still, Ashley was on medications from other doctors that she didn't tell her therapist. Defense used that against her, and in favor of Tom - saying it was entirely possible that Ashley Fallis could have written those suicide notes without telling her therapist.

When Ashley's parents were finally able to take the stand, they insisted that Ashley was fine throughout the night. Despite her miscarriage earlier in the day, Ashley was among family and friends. Her demeanor only changed when Tom became volatile. Jenna Fox described, once more, how Tom Fallis swore at them all and wished for them all to die before going into the bedroom and slamming the door.

Nick Glover also took the stand, repeating what he heard outside of his window that night. Tom Fallis' parents, however, denied that Tom had told them that he shot his wife. Kathy Glover also reiterated the phone call she got at one in the morning from Chelsey Arrigo. Unfortunately, when Arrigo took the stand, she couldn't remember making such a statement to Kathy Glover. All she remembered was hearing some arguing. Apparently, Arrigo was intoxicated because of her own New Year's celebration. Weld County Sheriff's Deputy, Chris Graves, was able to testify that he also heard with Nick Glover had heard that night, which was Tom Fallis admitting to shooting his wife. Still, he was questioned pretty hard after admitting that he should have come forward about it sooner than two years after the fact.

Forensic evidence didn't fair well in Ashley's favor, either. It was determined that the gunshot would very well could have been self inflicted. And yet, the prosecution called forward a forensic expert of their own, Jon Priest, who explained the exact opposite: no, Ashley's gunshot wound could not have been self inflicted.

There was so much testimony and evidence that the jury had to go through. The conflicting theories from the defense and the prosecution told two entirely different stories about what happened that night to Ashley Fallis. When the Jury retreated to deliberate the case and make their verdict, it didn't take them very long. In fact, the jury was only out for about three and a half hours. When they finally came back, Ashley's family could only wait with baited breath as the jury read out their decision.

Not guilty.

Tom Fallis was acquitted on the murder of his beloved wife, mother of his children. Ashley's family still holds their opinion that their daughter would never take her own life, and Justin Joseph maintains that the entire case of Ashley's death was handled poorly from start to finish. There was reasonable doubt that Ashley had killed herself that night, and there was no follow up done. Still, even after all the evidence was presented, the jury could not find Tom Fallis guilty. Whatever happened to Ashley Fallis that night will only ever be known by two people: Ashley and Tom.

THE MURDER OF BROOKE WILBERGER

55

OLIVIA WATSON

Chapter 1

May 24, 2004 is a day many people in Corvallis, Oregon will never forget. It was the day a drunk man who was also high on crack set forth to destroy a life. Joel Courtney set out that morning in his 1997 green Dodge Caravan in search of a young, pretty co-ed to fulfill his dark fantasies. He cruised through the Oregon State University campus, searching, failing. But Courtney was persistent, and his wishes were soon fulfilled after he came across the Oak Park apartment complex a block down the road.

On the same morning, Brooke Wilberger woke up without any inclination that this might be her final day on Earth. She was newly home after finishing her first year of University, and was enjoying how sunny the spring had turned out to be. She headed over to the Oak Park apartment complex, which her sister managed, to help do some cleaning and basic repairs. Her sister needed help washing the lightposts out in the parking lot, so Wilberger grabbed some rags and a bucket of soapy water and got to work.

A few minutes into her work, Wilberger noticed a green van pull up. Inside, a man was waving an envelope at her, trying to get her attention. He looked like he needed help, so Wilberger approached. When the van pulled away seconds later, all that was left of Brooke was the soapy water and her now-broken flip flops.

It would be more than five years before Brooke Wilberger came home, but she would never come home alive. The story of her disappearance was a twisted tale full of hope, but it would only ever have a bittersweet ending.

Chapter 2

Brooke Wilberger was born in Fresno, California on February 20, 1985. She was the youngest of six. With three older sisters and two older brothers, she lived in a busy household, but it was a pleasant place to live. Her parents, Greg and Cammy Wilberger, were devout

Mormons, and raised their children to be the same. The family was incredibly close-knit.

Brooke Wilberger grew to be quite a beautiful, accomplished young woman. Besides boasting a strong set of mormon morals, she also excelled in school and had a lot of friends. The tall, thin blonde also received a lot of attention from the guys in her school, but she seldom dated.

The summer before Brooke began high school, the Wilberger family left California behind and moved North to Eugene, Oregon. Here, Brooke attended Elmira High School, and met her first serious boyfriend, Justin Blake. Blake also came from a mormon family, and was devoted to his religion, so the couple got along famously. They respected each other's minds, bodies, and faith.

The young couple graduated together in 2003, and while they were both dedicated to each other, they were on different paths towards the future. Wilberger wanted to go right to college so she could better equip herself with the knowledge she would need to turn around and better those in need around her. Blake was ready to jump into missionary work.

Wilberger was accepted into the Brigham Young University in Provo, Utah, and when she set off for her freshman year there, Blake set off for Venezuela to participate in a Mormon missionary campaign.

Although she was separated from her first love, Wilberger could not deny how happy she was at Brigham Young. The University was owned and operated by the Church of Jesus Christ of Latter Day Saints, and was the largest religious university in the country. She was immersed in her faith in new experiences and knowledge. She was actively participating in something much larger than herself, and she loved it.

Wilberger kept in constant contact with her family while away at University. She would often call and tell them about what she was learning, who she was meeting, and what she was doing. Her favorite topic of conversation, though, was always the inspiration her surroundings gave her to do better for the world. Although she was excited to see her family after the end of the year, she was in no rush to leave the busy, bustling campus for small-town Oregon.

After finishing her classes for the year, Brooke returned home to her family in late April of 2004. Her parents still lived in Eugene, but she wanted to maintain some of her freedom, so Brooke often stayed with her sister, Stephanie, who lived an hour outside of Eugene in an apartment complex she managed in Corvallis.

Her family were ecstatic to have her back home, close by, where they believed she would be safe.

Chapter 3

On May 24, 2004, Brooke had been home for about a month. She was staying with her sister in the Oak Park apartments, which were just down the road from Oregon State University, where summer classes were already in full swing.

That morning, a female student of Oregon State named Randy was walking through the Reser Stadium parking lot when she noticed a green van driving around her. When it pulled up next to her, the driver of the van got out and asked Randy for directions. The student had a bad feeling about the man, and when she looked in the back seat of the van she noticed a bunch of empty boxes and blankets. Before the man could get too close, Randy excused herself and hurried off to class.

Several minutes later, another student, Crystal, was approached by the same van in the same parking lot. Crystal did speak to the man, who again asked for directions, but the conversation was interrupted by an athletic's coach, who Randy had reported the earlier incident to. When confronted by the coach, the van's driver quickly jumped back into his vehicle and sped off of the campus.

While this was all happening, Brooke Wilberger was a block down the road from Reser Stadium at the Oak Park apartment complex. That morning she was planning on helping her sister Stephanie do some routine maintenance work on the complex. She decided to start with washing the lamp posts in the parking lot, so she grabbed a bucket, filled it with soapy water, and headed outside. Stephanie saw Brooke hard at work scrubbing the lamp posts at 10:00 a.m. It was the last time she ever saw her sister alive.

Shortly after 10:00 a.m., the same green van that had been causing havoc on the Oregon State campus pulled into the Oak Park apartment complex. The van pulled up to Brooke, blocking her view of the apartments. He began asking for directions, but when Brooke drew near, he pulled out a knife and forced the 19-year-old into the back seat of his van and sped away.

Five minutes down the road, the van pulled over and it's driver, Joel Courtney, got out and bound Wilberger's arms and legs with duct tape. He also covered her body with blankets he had stashed in the back seat. After this, he sped off towards a nearby area that was covered with heavy forestation.

Hours after Brooke was snatched from the apartment complex, her sister Stephanie realized that she hadn't seen or heard from her in a while. She decided to track her down to make sure she was okay, and began with the place she had last seen her—the complex's parking lot. When she got there she was surprised to see an almost empty parking lot, save for the cleaning supplies Brooke had been using and Brookes flip flop sandals, one of which was now broken.

Stephanie immediately ran inside and called police, who immediately launched a missing person's case despite their protocol stating they should wait 24-hours first. Brooke's broken flip flops at her last known location triggered enough of an alarm.

When detectives arrived at the Oak Park apartments, they quickly discovered that her truck, purse, phone, and wallet were all still at the apartments. If she had left the apartments by herself, she had done so without any identification, money, and shoes. It seemed unlikely that this would have been the case.

The search for Brooke began in the same way most crimes do—with the victim's significant other. In this case, Brooke's long-term boyfriend was quickly eliminated because he was over 4000 miles away doing missionary work in Venezuela. Brooke's family was also quickly ruled out.

During this process, the word of Brooke's disappearance quickly got out to the community, and a massive volunteer search was launched by the Wilberger's Mormon church. Within days of Brooke's disappearance, both Eugene and Corvallis were covered in missing posters detailing Brooke's physical appearance and last known location. Over 4000 acres of heavily-wooded area outside of Corvallis was searched for any signs of the missing girl over eleven days. None were found.

Police soon began to realize that the best chance they had of finding Wilberger would be to find the person who had taken her from the Oak Park apartments, so they quickly began to focus on the few early leads they had in the case.

The method in which Wilberger was abducted led police to believe that her abductor was a repeat offender. It's difficult to grab a grown woman off of the streets without anyone seeing or hearing anything. Police began looking through sex offender registries and crime logs to create a suspect pool, one that turned out to include over one thousand names, all of whom were interviewed.

One of the first people contacted by police was 45-year-old ex-con Lauren Hugo Krueger. He had been convicted in 1985 for attempted rape and had served time for the felony assault and kidnapping of a 23-year-old jogger. Krueger had also been questioned in relation to several reports of harassment and stalking. Most damningly, Krueger had also been spotted at a car dealership less than a block away from where Wilberger was abducted from. It was a promising start to the investigation.

Chapter 4

Many police officers in Corvallis believed they may have identified the man who abducted Brooke Wilberger on May 24, 2004, as being Lauren Krueger. He had committed several similar crimes in the past, making him a likely suspect. However, when he was interviewed, police discovered he had an airtight alibi for that afternoon, and he was eliminated in the case.

Shortly after Krueger was eliminated as a suspect, another man by the name of Sun Koo King was identified as a probably suspect. King was an Oregon State graduate who was unemployed and lived in the area. He had recently had a lot of trouble with the law for breaking and entering into Oregon State dorm rooms and stealing their occupants underwear.

Detectives searched King's home and found a startling collection of women's underwear, used tampons, and pubic hair. King also catalogued where he found each object of his collection, which allowed investigators to see that he had gotten most of the items from dorms at the University and from the laundry room at the Oak Park apartments, the same apartments Brooke Wilberger lived in with her sister.

Police were shocked by what they found at King's home, but what shocked them more was that there seemed to be no sign of Brooke Wilberger anywhere. Further, King passed a polygraph test and seemed to have an airtight alibi. Investigators were again forced to abandon the promising lead.

By October 2004, five months after Brooke's disappearance, police had a third strong suspect—Aeryn Evans. Evans had been arrested the month before for attacking a Oregon State student on campus. Evans' step sister called police after the incident suspecting that he may have been involved in Wilberger's disappearance too, but this was quickly discovered to be impossible by police.

Frustrated by having to eliminate three great suspects in a row, police decided they needed to take a different approach in the hunt for Wilberger's abductor. They decided to focus in on the one piece of evidence they had directly connected to the person who took Brooke—a green Dodge Caravan.

Police suspected that the green van was connected to Brooke's disappearance because of the two earlier reports from Randy and Crystal on the Oregon State campus, as well as from a tip call from a man who identified himself as Brian. Brian told police that he had seen a green van driving around the area Brooke was last seen. The driver was acting suspicious enough that the van had stood out to the man. The three incidents were too bizarre for police not to connect with Brooke's disappearance on the same day.

Both Randy and Crystal were interviewed by police, but neither were able to give a clear description of the van's driver. They had both been too spooked at the time. However, the coach that had intervened in Crystal's encounter with the van had gotten a good look at the van itself and was able to provide police with more details, including the fact that the van had had Minnesota license plates.

While police were now convinced that the van seen on the Oregon State University was the van used in Wilberger's abduction, they still had no idea where to find the van, and no idea who had been driving it. By November, 2004, six months after Brooke's abduction, investigators assigned to the case were still on square one. Little did they know though, that another crime was about to be committed in Albuquerque, New Mexico, and this crime would lead them right to Wilberger's killer.

Chapter 5

On November 29, 2004, a 22-year-old Russian exchange student, who goes by the pseudonym Natalie Kirov, left the daycare she worked at on the University of New Mexico campus for home. Minutes away from her doorstep, a car pulled up next to her and a man jumped out and told her to get into the car. Terrified, she complied.

The man held Kirov captive in his car at knifepoint as he drove off. When they got to a secluded area of a dead end road, the man pulled the car over and began to sexually assault the young woman, forcing her to remove her clothes in the process.

After sexually assaulting the Russian beauty, the man declared that he needed a drug fix, a "pick-me-up," and drove to a shady apartment complex to purchase some crack. He left Kirov in his car, bound up with her own shoelaces. While her captor was inside, Kirov managed to free her hands and unlock the car. She immediately ran into the street, despite being mostly naked, and flagged down a passing car.

Just as Kirov settles into the car she flagged down her captor emerged from the nearby apartment. After seeing how terrified Kirov became, her saviours quickly drove off in the opposite direction and brought her to the police station. She was finally safe.

Police immediately responded to Kirov's report by visiting the apartments her attacker stopped in to buy his drugs. They were able to find a lady willing to admit that a guy named Joel matching Kirov's description had stopped by earlier that night. Further, she knew where Joel lived.

Police immediately proceeded to the address given to them and immediately spotted the red car Kirov described parked in the lot outside. Police had just begun examining the vehicle when they were approached by a man who said he owned the car. Police asked him if his name was Joel, and he immediately responded yes. Police responded in turn by arresting him.

The Joel police now had in custody was Joel Courtney—a 38-year-old mechanic fisherman. Joel lived in Albuquerque with his wife and three children, but his marriage was incredibly unstable. Only a few weeks before this arrest, Courtney's wife had taken out a restraining order on him.

When police dug deeper into Courtney's past, they discovered that he had a long standing drug problem that they were able to trace back to his childhood in Beaverton, Oregon. Courtney had grown up an average, loving family, but his life began deteriorating after he started using drugs at the tender age of 11. By the age of 14, Courtney began repeatedly molesting his sister and cousins, and by the age of 19, he began experimenting with satanism, and was arrested several times for sexual assaults.

Now, many years later, he was back in custody for the sexual assault of Natalie Kirov, but it had been almost 20 years since he had been committed a crime, something Albuquerque detectives were skeptical of. They wondered if he had victimized any other women who crossed his path over the years, so they contacted authorities in Oregon, Courtney's home state, to ask if there were any unsolved crimes that matched Courtney's modis operandi. Almost immediately, Oregon police mentioned the disappearance of Brooke Wilberger six months ago, hoping to finally provide some answers to Wilberger's family and the surrounding communities.

Chapter 6

After having Joel Courtney brought to their attention, the Brooke Wilberger taskforce in Corvallis, Oregon decided to look further into Courtney's past to see if they could connect him to Wilberger's disappearance. They were quickly rewarded for this decision.

Investigators soon found out that Courtney and his wife had only recently moved to Albuquerque, New Mexico. Before that, the couple moved around Oregon frequently looking for cheap accommodations. At the time of Wilberger's disappearance, the couple were living with relatives in Portland, Oregon, an hour's drive away from Corvallis.

Further, investigators found that Courtney had been working for a janitorial company in Corvallis while he lived in Portland. He drove the company's 1997 green Dodge Caravan with Minnesota license plates to and from work each day.

Courtney's van was the exact van police had been trying to track down for the last several months. Armed with this knowledge, police managed to track down the vehicle, which was immediately brought to Portland to be searched for any forensic evidence that may have survived. Specifically, they were looking for any DNA evidence to compare to known samples of Brooke Wilberger and Joel Courtney himself.

While investigators waited for the DNA results to come back from the lab, they looked into Courtney's whereabouts the day Brooke Wilberger disappeared. They discovered that Joel Courtney had actually been expected in court to face a DUI charge that very day.

Police learned that on this day Courtney apparently made a call from Corvallis saying he would be late for his court time, but he never appeared. Police also learned that the next day, a disheveled Courtney had shown up at a family member's house 16-hours away from Corvallis. When asked why he was in such a state, Courtney came up with a story of how he ran into a gang of men in the woods who had captured a young woman and forced him to do terrible things he did not want to do. Amazingly, the family member chalked the unbelievable story to Courtney's chronic drug use, and never asked about it again.

On the one-year anniversary of Brooke Wilberger's disappearance, Corvallis investigators finally received the results of the forensic sweep of the green Dodge Caravan. It was worth the wait.

The evidence recovered from the van conclusively proved that not only had both Brooke Wilberger and Joel Courtney been in the green van, but Joel Courtney had been the person to place Wilberger there, and he likely knew where she was now. The final challenge investigators now had was getting Courtney to reveal this information so they could finally bring Brooke home.

Chapter 7

On August 2, 2005, Joel Courtney, who is preparing to go on trial for the kidnap and sexual assault of Natalie Kirov is served an arrest warrant for the kidnap and presumptive murder of Brooke Wilberger. Weeks later, the Kirov case is brought to trial, and faced with the indisputable evidence against him, Courtney pleaded guilty. He was given a sentence of 18 years in prison.

But Joel Courtney didn't have long to get settled in the New Mexico prison system. In April of 2008, he was extradited to Oregon in order to stand on trial for the charges laid against him in Brooke Wilberger's case.

When the trial began in Spring of 2009, the prosecutors in the case showed the court Joel Courtney's long standing history of sexual assaults against women, which dated back to his late teen years. They also presented a witness that had seen Courtney the night before Wilberger's abduction. This individual stated that they used to work together, and that they had spent the night of May 23, 2004, drinking and smoking crack together.

Although prosecutors had a large amount of evidence against Courtney, they were missing something very important, something desired not only by them but also by Wilberger's family and the entire community of Corvallis and Eugene—Brooke.

Up to this point, investigators had been unable to find any indication of Brooke's final resting place, and Courtney wasn't about to give this information up easily. The Wilberger family was all but begging the prosecutors and investigators working on Brooke's case to make a deal with Courtney so they could bring their daughter home and give her a peaceful burial.

The District Attorney eventually succumbed to the Wilbergers' wishes and presented a plea deal to Joel Courtney. The terms of the plea deal stated that Courtney needed to plead guilty to all charges against him and reveal the location of Brooke's remains. In exchange, Courtney would receive life in prison without parole.

Courtney rejected this initial offer, but quickly returned to the bargaining table. Courtney offered to plead guilty to the crime if he could be locked up in New Mexico near his family instead of in

Oregon. He also promised to reveal the location of Brooke Wilberger's remains. Courtney's counter-offer was accepted and signed.

To uphold his side of the plea deal, Joel Courtney drew a map to Brooke's burial site for investigators and walked them through the events of May 24, 2004. He told investigators the story of how he forced the young woman into his van and took her to some nearby woods to sexually assault her. After being raped, Wilberger became enraged, and tried to fight her way to freedom. Courtney responded by punching Wilberger until she fell unconscious before beating her to her certain death with a piece of wood he found nearby.

Based on this confession, and armed with Courtney's map, investigators drove 10 miles outside of Corvallis to a heavily wooded area known as the Coast Range. Their goal: to locate Brooke's remains.

After several days of searching, investigators were finally able to locate Brooke Wilberger's remains in a shallow grave next to a clearing of trees. Her grave was hidden beneath a mound of tree branches and leaves. For the Wilbergers, the news was bittersweet. They finally knew what happened to their daughter, and they finally could bring her home, but up until this point they had always maintained hope that when she came home she would still be alive.

Joel Courtney was formally sentenced to life in prison without parole two months later, and was brought back to a New Mexico prison where he prepared to spend the rest of his days. It was the end of a violent sexual predator's freedom, but most importantly, it was the end of the mystery that had plagued Oregon police and Brooke Wilberger's friends and family for years.

Brooke was finally home and at peace, and the world was a little safer now with Joel Courtney now behind bars. This is little solace to those who continue to miss Brooke Wilberger dearly, but having some answers is inarguably better than none. Those who knew Brooke in life remember her as the sweet, caring angel she was. She had a good soul in her heart and a good head on her shoulders and would have undoubtedly achieved great things in life.

Brooke's family still keep in contact with the investigators that dedicated their time to bringing Brooke home—they attend the officers' retirement parties and exchange the occasional email—a small token of the gratitude they will always hold.

THE MURDER OF CAROL TAGGART

OLIVIA WATSON

On Boxing Day of 2014, a young man living in Fife, Scotland walks into the local police station to inquire about his missing mother, Carol Taggart. The young man is her son, Ross. Carol Taggart has been missing for three days. Her family is desperately worried, apart from Ross, who is still going out clubbing and hitting the town using Carol's credit cards.

Then police find Carol's body, devastating her daughter Lorraine and partner Shaun.

Growing up, the Taggart family were incredibly close. The family comprised of four members, Carol, the mom, Shaun, the dad, and Ross and Lorraine, who were brother and sister.

Ross is four years older than Lorraine and had a different father, but that never mattered to them. The two were very close as children, and Ross always looked out for his sister. Both were loved and cared for by Shaun and Carol.

Lorraine, who was both Shaun and Carol's biological child, was very close with her father. She was a daddy's girl. Likewise, Ross was a momma's boy, and proud of it. Ross and Carol shared a very close relationship, but Shaun always considered Ross to be his son through and through, and to Ross, Shaun was always dad. The two shared many happy father-son memories. Shaun had taught Ross how to ride a bike when he was younger; he had been there to take the training wheels off. They were a typical family of four.

Carol and her son shared a special closeness. Although there was always enough love for Lorraine, there was no denying that Ross had always been the favorite when it came to Carol. There was always a little bit extra love for Ross.

In his mother's eyes, Ross could do no wrong. To her, he couldn't lie, he couldn't cheat. Her family described her as believing that the sun simply shone out of Ross's backside. He was the golden boy.

But in his teenage years, Ross went through some significant changes. As a child, he'd always been a loving, supportive brother and son. He was outgoing, loved to meet new people, and always seemed to be smiling. When he got older, he became very introverted.

As a young adult, Ross never said much. He wasn't a man of many words. When he was displeased, he wouldn't speak up. He would just give an unmistakable look, and his friends and family would instantly know.

For his family especially, this was frustrating. They couldn't get into his psyche, or figure out what he was thinking. They would ask him why he behaved certain ways, but they would never get clear answers from him. Most of the time, they wouldn't get answers at all. Ross would simply give them a blank stare and go to hide in his room, isolated from the family and the rest of the world.

Ross knew he didn't need to work hard to be loved by his family though. He knew he was the perfect child in his mother's eyes, he'd always known it, since the day he was born. The pair had had years together to bond before Shaun and Lorraine entered their lives. They had a mutual feeling that it had always been just the two of them.

Ross was well aware of this connection, and he used it to his advantage. He used his mother's affection against her often, emotionally manipulating her to get his way. To those around Ross and Carol, Ross's behavior showed him to be lazy, unfair, and rude. He was a user and a narcissist. But to Carol, he was none of these things. He needed her, he was her only son, and he relied on her for everything. Ross eloquently played on every emotion Carol had.

Ross was lazy in life and expected everything to land in his lap. He was brought up in a beautiful house, went on beautiful holidays, and had beautiful cars. He was used to getting everything he wanted, so he saw no point in trying to work for anything. That seemed to be his outlook on life—why try when you know it will be provided anyways.

Ross's laziness wasn't a product of his upbringing. Lorraine, Ross's sister, grew up with all the same luxuries as him, but as an adult, she worked hard to make her parents proud. She understood the privileges she had and used them to better her life and become independent. Ross was the opposite.

In the eyes of her father, Lorraine was a roaring success. She worked hard in school, achieved high grades, held down jobs, and went off to college to study dancing, which had been a lifelong passion for her. While this was happening, Ross was at home cruising through life, spending most of it alone in his room or with Carol.

Carol always saw the best in Ross. She saw Ross's laziness as a struggle. She worked hard to please him, to make him know that he was her priority. Ross knew this. He knew he could use those feelings to make his mom support him financially. More than that though, Ross understood that he could play up his role as the helpless son to draw Carol away from other people who saw him differently, especially their family.

Carol defended Ross to no end when others tried to make Carol see she was being taken advantage of, but that wasn't enough for Ross. He wanted to isolate her. He wanted to be her entire world so the money and affection would never stop.

Carol and Shaun had very different ideas of how to deal with Ross behavior as he aged. Shaun wanted to be hard on their son. He believed that Ross, who was now in his early 20's, was old enough to learn how to hold down a job and stand on his own two feet. He thought coddling Ross was holding him back from being an independent adult, but Carol wouldn't hear it. She believed that it would just take time for Ross to come out of his slump. He would grow into a responsible adult; he just wasn't ready yet.

Shaun and Carol began constantly arguing about what to do with Ross. He had begun driving a massive wedge in between his parents. For years the couple argued, unable to come to any resemblance of an agreement on how to deal with their overgrown child. While Shaun was still adamant that Ross needed to become more independent, Carol began to aggressively prioritize her son above all else, even going as far as telling Shaun that Ross came before everything, including Shaun.

After 19 years together, Shaun and Carol separated. It was becoming clear to both of them that they were no longer on the same page in life, and there was no end to their fighting in sight. Both Shaun and Lorraine blamed Ross entirely for the separation.

Shaun was heartbroken by the separation, but there didn't seem to be anything he could do. He couldn't sit back and watch the woman he loved get taken advantage of by her son, especially when he was expected to submit to Ross's wishes as well. Reluctantly, he decided to move out of the family's house.

Now, the Taggart household consisted of Carol, Ross, and Lorraine. While Lorraine was saddened by the departure of her father, Ross was elated. He loved being the man of the house. Lorraine was disturbed by the new dynamic that was developing at home and left as soon as she could. She later described the two years where it was just the three of them together as the longest two years of her life.

After her separation from Shaun, Carol began suffering from bouts of depression, so much so that she was unable to disguise her sadness from her children. In her vulnerable state, Carol was even less prepared to stand up against Ross, who began exploiting her even more.

It was around this time that Lorraine began to understand the kind of person her older brother had developed into. He wasn't a lazy boy with no ambition; he was a user. He was bleeding his mother dry. Lorraine tried to warn her mom that Ross was taking advantage of her, but par for the course, she wouldn't listen. Lorraine was terrified that Ross was going to turn against Carol one day and that Carol would be left with nothing.

Lorraine tried to get her mother help for her depression. The more depressed Carol got, the more dependent on Ross she became, and Lorraine could recognize that that was a recipe for disaster. She went to appointment after appointment with Carol and tried to get her enlisted in different facilities. But this didn't help, Carol's depression got progressively worse. She was lost.

Lorraine recalls feeling incredibly frustrated with her brother during this time. While she was doing everything she could to try and help her mom, he continued to prey on her weaknesses. And for whatever reason, Carol continued to rely on Ross more and more, ignoring Lorraine's pleas and attempts to get her help. Lorraine couldn't crack through the glass that separated herself from Ross and Carol's relationship. As hard as she tried, she was always on the outside looking in.

After years of this, Lorraine couldn't take it anymore. She relented to the fact that Ross was always going to come first in his mother's eyes, and that there was little she could do about this. All she could do was try to make her mother proud by succeeding in her own life, and it was time for Lorraine to focus on this. She couldn't keep fighting a losing battle, so she left home.

Finally, Ross had his mother all to himself. Although at this point in his life, Ross was in his mid-twenties, he had no serious relationships outside of his relationship with his mother. He had cycled through a series of girlfriends, but unsurprisingly, none of them stuck around for long.

Carol, in her depressed state, also had a hard time maintaining relationships outside of Ross. She had no interest in dating, as she still had a strong love for Shaun, and she had little motivation to make or maintain friendships.

Carol and Ross's relationship developed into a non-sexual partnership. The two began going on holidays alone together, and they began spending all their social time together, it was the kind of relationship you would expect to see between a husband and a wife—not a mother and a son.

The more time the pair spent together, the more fused their lives became. Carol was now fully dependant on her son emotionally, but

Ross was still only using his mother to make gains for his own life, and Carol was completely unable to see this for herself.

Although the family of four had been close when Lorraine and Ross were younger, there was now a clear divide. While Ross and Carol were perfectly happy in their closeness, both Lorraine and Shaun found it incredibly strange. And they were no longer alone. Many friends and family members of Carol began questioning Ross's motives. There were very few people outside of Carol that saw Ross as a good man. To most, he was a bad apple.

When Ross recognized that his mother had become fully dependent on him, he began to exert dominant control over her. He no longer felt the need to be sneaky in his manipulations; he was comfortable being outright aggressive with Carol. When she disagreed with Ross or said no to him, he would get angry and withdraw, knowing she would work hard to get back in his good books, giving him everything he had asked for initially and more.

Lorraine saw the shift in her brother's attitude towards their mom and grew increasingly concerned. He was becoming nasty. His tone when he argued with Carol was sharp, condescending, and cruel. It sent the message that he was going to get his way no matter what.

Even though Shaun had been driven out of the family home by Ross, he continued to see Carol. The pair began to grow closer again, and Shaun worked to pry Carol away from Ross just a little bit. For a while, it looked like it was working. Shaun and Carol had grown very close again, and Shaun asked to move back in, thinking they had finally found a way to mend their broken relationship. But things did not go as planned. Before Shaun could move back in, Carol told him that she'd have to ask Ross for permission.

This set Shaun off. Throughout their separation, Shaun had continued to help Carol financially support herself and their children, as her depression had been making it difficult for Carol to work consistently. Shaun helped pay the bills; Ross did not. And Shaun and

Carol were adults. He saw no reason why Ross had any say in the matter. Shaun never moved back into the family home.

On August 11, 2012, Lorraine married her husband on a beautiful sunny day. It was the happiest day of her life, and one of the last happy day the whole family would ever spend together. Shaun proudly walked Lorraine down the aisle, and Carol, elated to be the mother of such a beautiful bride, was too swept up in the magic of the moment to care about Ross's dislike of her re-budding relationship with Shaun. The family was able to celebrate together openly. After this day though, Ross began to isolate his mother from the rest of the family further, something they all thought was impossible. When Lorraine had her first child a year later, Carol wasn't allowed to visit and see her first grandchild for over six months.

In October of 2014, Carol took Ross on vacation to New York City for his thirtieth birthday. Most people at the age of thirty have moved out of their parents' home, have started a career, and possibly even a family. But Ross's life couldn't have been more of the opposite, and he was pleased as punch about that. After they returned from their trip, Carol continued to indulge her son, spending over £1,500 on Christmas presents to give to him before the day even arrived. Unbeknownst to her at the time, Carol would never see Christmas that year.

Out of the blue, on December 23, 2014, Ross Taggart called the Fife police to report Carol missing. He told the operator on the other end of the line that he had gotten into an argument with his mom and she had simply walked out of the house. Because she had been suffering from bouts of depression for years now, he was worried that she had taken the argument too much to heart and had gone and done something terrible.

Investigators charged with looking into Carol's disappearance had several concerns about the nature of this phone call. While Ross sounded confident on the phone, he didn't sound worried.

Additionally, he had made a point of getting information across that isn't common when people usually report family members as missing. He seemed to be trying to set up a specific scenario; it was suggestive and manipulative. Unfortunately for Ross, manipulating the police was not as easy as manipulating his mother. Investigators were wary of Ross from the moment he picked up the phone.

Lorraine had not spoken to Ross in a very long time when she got a missed call from him while out shopping with her husband. She was nervous about why he was calling, so her husband called him back on her behalf. That's when Ross told them the news—Carol was missing.

Initially, Lorraine wasn't too worried. She was hopeful that Carol had merely begun to see Ross for who he was and needed to take some space from him and therefore wasn't answering his calls. She figured she would call her mom later, and Carol would see that it was Lorraine and she would answer. By the end of the day, Lorraine had called her mother over ten times but had received no answer. That's when she began to feel an overwhelming sense of dread.

Lorraine thought of several possible scenarios of why Carol had run off and wasn't answering her calls, and they all seemed to revolve around Carol's relationship with Ross. The most likely, she thought, was that Ross had hit Carol, and Carol had gone into hiding to protect him. Despite how little she liked her brother, Lorraine still never expected the truth to be what it was.

In the days after he reported his mother missing, Ross was closely watched by the police. His movements and actions were caught on CCTV cameras and were being monitored. In the late hours of Christmas Eve, he was seen walking around the caravan park where his mother owned a holiday caravan. A few hours later he was seen withdrawing cash using his mother's card. Even later that same night, he was seen buying drinks at a nightclub, again on his mother's dime.

After Christmas Eve came and went without a word from Carol, Lorraine began to heavily doubt her brother's account of what had happened right before their mother went missing. On Christmas Day, she got a call from the police. They had found Carol's car with her purse, wallet, and phone inside. At that point, they knew something terrible had happened. They knew she was gone.

On December 26, three days after reporting his mother missing, Ross went into the local police station to check in on how the investigation was going. The visit was captured on camera and showed the true lack of emotion Ross was exhibiting during this time. This visit raised further red flags regarding Ross's involvement in Carol's disappearance. There was no recognition of sadness in Ross as he eagerly asked questions about what the police had found out so far. He wanted to know exactly what the police knew, which made them feel like he was trying to figure out something more specific—were they on to him.

Ross's actions after his mother disappeared were suspicious to everyone around him. While his sister Lorraine and father Shaun were at home crying their eyes out, calling people, and trying to wrap their brains around what was happening, Shaun was carrying out his life seemingly as normal. He continued to go out to clubs and use his mother's cards on a regular basis, even buying movie tickets to see *The Hunger Games* at the cinema. He sold Carol's expensive jewelry, justifying the act by saying he was entitled to her estate according to her will. He was not acting as if he'd just lost the person who meant everything to him just a week ago.

By January 1, 2015, Ross was the sole target of the investigation into Carol Taggart's disappearance. The rest of Carol's family had picked up on this, as he had quickly become a topic of interest when police questioned them. Initially, it was just about Ross's behavior in the days following Carol's disappearance, questions like why is he still going out clubbing? Does he have permission to use Carol's cards?

But as time passed, investigators got less subtle with their questions. Eventually, they got to the meat of their queries and asked

Lorraine and Shaun the same question separately: do you think Ross would do something to Carol? Their answer was the same—absolutely.

On January 11, 2015, the Taggart family received the news they had all been dreading: Carol's body had been found.

Carol's body was found stashed beneath a caravan in the same park as Carol's. It was the same place Ross had been seen on CCTV footage stalking around on Christmas Eve. Her body told a horrifying story to police, a story of brutal violence at the hands of someone with nothing but hate in their hearts. She had been battered to death and throttled. Her neck had been broken, and she was covered in bruises. The damage was so horrific that when Lorraine was brought in to identify the body, she was only shown her mother's wrist, which had a distinctive tattoo on it, although decomposition hadn't yet made her face unrecognizable.

To both police and the rest of the Taggart family, Ross was the prime suspect. Above all else, Lorraine was angered that even in death, Ross discarded their mother. She was left outside alone, where it was cold and wet. He didn't make a mistake. He did not feel guilty. He had left the only person in the world who loved him outside in the cold alone for over two weeks, and he didn't seem the least bit sorry.

Three days after police found Carol's body, Ross was formally arrested and charged with his mother's murder. Lorraine and Shaun felt relief for the first time in weeks when they heard the news. It was unfair to them that Ross was allowed to live freely after taking the life of their loved one. They hoped that at least they could now get some answers from Ross on how he was able to commit such a terrible act.

As well as being charged with murder, Ross was also charged with perverting the course of justice after lying to police and taking measures to prevent investigators from discovering what had happened to his mother.

During his trial, which took place in Edinburgh in November 2015, the severity of Ross's attack on his mother became clear to Shaun and Lorraine for the first time. He had beaten his mother with his fists so severely that he had partially broken her neck. He then strangled her so violently that her neck snapped the rest of the way. It wasn't a crime committed from a distance. It wasn't cold and calculated. It had been done with his own bare hands, face-to-face with the woman who raised him, while she screamed out in pain and fought for her life. It was a lengthy, sustained attack, after which he wrapped her body in a sheet, put her in the trunk of her own car, and drove her out to her caravan where she stayed for several days before he went back and buried her beneath a neighboring caravan.

The case against Ross was overwhelming. Everything pointed towards him. The prosecution had been able to assemble hours of suspicious activities captured by CCTV cameras along with 188 witnesses and experts. Including Ross, the defense only presented two.

Just when the family thought they had heard the worst though, the prosecution presented a surprise witness whose purpose was to demonstrate further the lack of remorse Ross had for what he had done.

The witness was a young woman, who neither Lorraine nor Shaun had ever seen before. They soon heard that she had been contacted by Ross through the online dating app Plenty of Fish the night that he had murdered Carol. He was using the app to look for casual sex just hours after dumping his mother's body, unbeknownst to the young woman. To prove that the young woman was telling the truth, prosecutors presented the GPS log from Carol's vehicle. Both the locations of Carol's caravan and the young woman's house appeared on the log in succession.

As well as condemning Ross beyond a reasonable doubt, this information also provided insight into Ross's mindset the night he killed his mother. He was not remorseful in the least. He had felt powerful, dominant, and wanted to continue the adrenaline high he got from committing murder. He wasn't a normal human being—he was a psychopathic narcissist.

Despite the overwhelming amount of evidence against him, Ross took the stand in his own defense and denied having anything to do with the disappearance or murder of his mother. He stuck to the story he told police over the phone when he first reported her missing—she had simply stormed off into the night after an argument. His family, watching from the court, recognized the blank look on his face he always wore when he lied.

The jury in the case took less than an hour to reach a unanimous verdict of guilty on all charges. Ross received a life sentence, which meant he would spend a minimum of 18 years in jail. To Lorraine and Shaun, this was barely justice. He was set to be released from prison at a younger age than Carol had been when she died.

Carol's memory lives on in the hearts of Shaun and Lorraine, but their hearts will be forever broken. Carol had so much love in her, and it was incredibly difficult to see her taken away from them by the person that she loved the most. Ross had been her golden boy, she had given him everything she had and more, and just as those around her feared, Ross took everything from Carol. He took her money, her love, and ultimately, her life.

THE MURDER OF DOMINIQUE DUNNE

ERICA THOMAS

Destined for stardom

In November 1959, film producer Dominick Dunne and actress Ellen (Lenny) Dunne welcomed a new baby to their growing family. Dominique Dunne was the couple's youngest of three children, and their only daughter. Dunne and her older brothers grew up surrounded by the arts – in addition to the influence of their parents, who were active in the California film industry, the children were frequently surrounded by celebrities of the 50s and 60s – close family friends who were often guests at the family home.

Dunne and her siblings grew up in a large house in Beverly Hills, but moved around fairly frequently as Dunne attended schools across the country – in Los Angeles, Connecticut, and Colorado. However, Dunne's childhood wasn't entirely carefree – when she was just eleven years old, Dunne's parents divorced. A few years later, in 1975, her mother was diagnosed with multiple sclerosis.

Still, Dunne pursued her education. After her graduation in 1977, Dunne studied art and Italian in Florence, at the Michelangelo School and at the British Institute. When she returned to California, she worked briefly as a receptionist and translator for Los Angeles' Italian Trade Commission before venturing back to Ft. Collins to study acting at the Colorado State University.

Her studies in Colorado were short-lived, however, and Dunne left after only one year to start auditioning back in California. Just a few weeks later, she was offered her very first film role. Dunne's acting career took off quite quickly – in her first three years, Dunne appeared as a guest on many well-known television shows, including *Family*, *CHiPs*, and *Fame*. And after taking on roles in four made-for-TV movies, Dunne made her cinematic debut as Dana Freeling in the movie "Poltergeist."

"One day, she decided to become an actress and the next week she was on a back lot making a movie, and that from then on she never stopped," said Dunne's father Dominick in a piece he wrote for Vanity

Fair in March 1984. "She loved being an actress and was passionate about her career."

"At ease in a sophisticated world."

To her friends and family, Dunne was known as a friendly, kind person. Despite having grown up with wealth and fame, Dunne's father described her as "totally at ease in a sophisticated world without being sophisticated herself." Indeed, Dunne dressed in casual clothes, preferring jeans and t-shirts to the upscale fashions her peers sported – and drove a blue Volkswagen Bug convertible.

Dunne loved cooking, traveling, baseball, and languages – particularly Italian, which she continued to speak quite fluently. She also loved animals, and had a soft spot for unwanted strays. Dunne adopted a cat with a lobotomy, a large dog with stunted legs, a snake, and a rabbit, among many other cats and dogs.

Even before her role in "Poltergeist," Dunne was a firm believer in supernatural phenomena, and friends say she was strictly superstitious.

Instant attraction

Dunne met John Thomas Sweeney in 1981, when she was twenty-two and he was twenty-five. Sweeney worked as a chef at Los Angeles' trendy "Ma Maison" restaurant, and Dunne was immediately drawn to him. After their initial introduction at a party that autumn, the pair quickly fell into a romantic relationship – and moved in together only a few weeks later, into a rental house in West-Hollywood.

However, their passion soon resulted in the first of many quarrels between the couple. Dunne was, by that point, well-known in Hollywood – a popular girl with many friends. Sweeney, on the other hand, had grown up poor in Pennsylvania, the product of a troubled family life. Despite Dunne's attempts to include him in her world, Sweeney felt like an outsider and was ashamed of his uncultured family history.

While Dunne had grown up with a loving family that respected and addressed emotional issues, Sweeney was raised in a coal town with an alcoholic father who, his mother claimed, often dealt with his frustrations by beating her – often in front of their children. By the time he was fourteen years old, his parents had divorced, and his father had developed epilepsy.

"Bitterly ashamed of his family and filled with a sense of worthlessness because he was a member of it, (Sweeney) longed to escape into a larger and more exciting life," read an article published in *People* magazine in 1983.

Sweeney's desire for a better life led him to pursue a culinary arts diploma from a local community college. At the age of twenty, he crossed the country to California, where he landed a job working at a restaurant called "Picolo's." Only one year later, he started as a chef's apprentice at "Ma Maison."

He was a talented, ambitious chef – and was willing to put in the work to achieve his career goals. After two years of double shifts, Sweeney was given a leave of absence to spend a year working on the French Riviera before returning to "Ma Maison" – where he worked as chef Wolfgang Puck's chief assistant.

His position at the glamorous restaurant gave him an opportunity to get a first-hand look at the elegant world he so desperately wanted to be a part of. And, after meeting Dunne, he finally felt like he would be able to access it. However, along with his excitement at being with a talented Hollywood actress, there was fear and insecurity – and the lasting sense of worthlessness he felt as a result of his troubled family life.

His jealousy started to take hold of the relationship. His interactions with Dunne grew more patronizing and dominating, and he began showing up on sets where Dunne was working to intimidate her male colleagues. Eventually, even that wasn't enough – Sweeney started to come to Dunne's rehearsals and even her acting classes.

It seemed Dunne couldn't do anything on her own without having to first discuss it with her boyfriend, which usually resulted in an argument that Dunne would never win. The more Dunne resisted Sweeney's possessiveness and jealousy, the more frightened he would be that she would ultimately reject him. Often, this fear would become anger.

"Alex said he was scary."

Dunne had introduced Sweeney to her family during the summer of 1982, flying the two of them out to New York where most of her family lived. According Dominick's article in Vanity Fair, Dunne's brother Alex was the only one who had "voiced his dislike" of her new boyfriend.

"Although I could see that Sweeney was excessively devoted to her, there was something off-putting about him," Dominick said.

The first night, Alex told his father about an incident that had happened after Dominick had left the restaurant. Dunne had been recognized by a man in the bar, who called out her iconic line from the film "Poltergeist." According to Alex, "there was no flirtation," just an excited, if slightly tipsy, fan.

"When Sweeney returned to the table and saw the man talking to (Dunne), he became enraged. He picked up the man and shook him," stated Dominick. "Alex said that Sweeney's reaction was out of all proportion to the incident going on. Alex said he was scary."

The next day, Dominick was to meet Dunne and Sweeney for lunch. Although he said he arrived at the restaurant late, the couple still wasn't there – and Dominick was already on his second bottle of Perrier by the time his daughter showed up with her boyfriend.

"I was immediately aware that she had been crying, and that there was tension between them," Dominick said. "The lunch was not a success. I found Sweeney ill at ease, nervous, difficult to talk to. It occurred to me that (Dunne) might have difficulty extricating herself from such a person, but I did not pursue the thought."

Getting physical

As the couple began fighting more and more, Sweeney's reactions frequently turned violent. On August 27, 1982, Sweeney reportedly tore out handfuls of Dunne's hair after grabbing it and using it to knock her head repeatedly against the floor. Dunne managed to get away from Sweeney and fled to her mother Lenny's house, with Sweeney following close behind. While Dunne's mother refused him entry and even threatened to call the police, it was only a few days before Dunne forgave her boyfriend and returned to their home.

Despite Dunne's forgiveness, Sweeney attacked her again not even a month later. On September 26, during another argument, Sweeney grabbed Dunne by the neck and pushed her to the floor before he started to choke her. Luckily, a friend heard the loud gagging noises coming from the next room – "it was the worst sound I had ever heard" – and came in to break up the fight.

"He tried to kill me!" Dunne cried out. Sweeney denied her accusation, insisting that Dunne come back to bed. Instead, she went into the bathroom, where she escaped out a window to spend the night with a friend.

The next day, Dunne showed up at the set of *Hill Street Blues*, where she was to guest star as an abuse victim for an episode of the show. According to accounts from cast and crew on the set, the bruises on Dunne's face and neck were "realistic" enough that she hardly needed any make-up for her role.

Dunne spent the following days in hiding, trying to avoid the abusive, angry boyfriend who was searching for her. Eventually, she contacted him to end the relationship – and to demand he leave the home they rented together so she could live there alone. Still, knowing how unpredictably angry and violent Sweeney could be, Dunne changed the locks of the house before moving back in without him.

The final battle

That autumn, Dunne had taken on a new role – playing Robin Maxwell for the three-episode science fiction miniseries *V.* She'd completed filming the scenes for the first episode and was nearly finished with the second episode on October 30, when she invited her co-star David Packer to rehearse scenes together at her home.

The pair were hard at work when Sweeney called Dunne at around 8:30 p.m. – and then showed up at the house only ten minutes later. Dunne answered the door with the chain fastened, but Sweeney demanded she come out and speak with him. Packer asked if he should leave, sensing Dunne's discomfort with the situation, but she said she wanted him to stay while she stepped outside to deal with her ex-boyfriend.

Out on the driveway, an argument broke out. Sweeney was pleading with Dunne to forgive him and take him back, but Dunne refused. She'd reached her limit and was no longer willing to tolerate Sweeney's anger and violence. Like he'd done before, Sweeney suddenly reached out and grabbed her firmly by the neck, dragging her up along the driveway into the next-door neighbour's back yard.

Dunne was no match for Sweeney – the petite actress was a mere 5'1" and 112 pounds. Sweeney, 6'1" and close to 200 pounds, held her down and began to strangle her. She was unable to fight him off, and eventually fell unconscious.

Meanwhile, Packer watched the confrontation with growing fear – he could see Sweeney's obvious rage and jealousy. When he heard screams followed by a thud, he called the police, only to be informed that the location was outside of the department's jurisdiction. After hanging up with the officer, Packer called a friend and left a message on his answering machine explaining that if he was found dead, John Sweeney should be held responsible.

Eventually, Packer went outside to check on Dunne, and found her lying on the driveway with Sweeney crouched next to her. Sweeney asked Dunne to call the police, and this time, they said they would send an officer. When the police arrived and found Dunne still unconscious, they called an ambulance, which arrived only five minutes later.

Brain-dead

On the way to the nearby Cedars Sinai Hospital, Dunne's heart came to a full stop, but doctors were able to restart it once the ambulance arrived. However, examinations showed that Dunne had sustained extensive damage from the anoxaemia during her strangulation – and that although her heart had been restarted, there was no way for doctors to reverse the death of her brain.

"There were tubes in her everywhere, and the life-support system caused her to breathe in and out with a grotesque jerking movement that seemed a parody of life," Dominick recalled. "Her eyes were open, massively enlarged, staring lifelessly up at the ceiling. Her beautiful hair had been shaved off. A large bolt had been screwed into her skull to relieve the pressure on her brain. Her neck was purpled and swollen; vividly visible on it were the marks of the massive hands of the man who had strangled her.

It was nearly impossible to look at her, but also impossible to look away."

The hospital's staff did everything they could for Dunne, and after five days, her parents made the decision to remove her from the life-support systems that were keeping her alive. Dunne died instantly, and her heart and kidneys were donated to the hospital to be used for transplants.

Dunne's tragic death was a shock to the entire Hollywood community, particularly for Dunne's extensive network of family and friends. Hundreds of people attended Dunne's funeral, held on November 6 at the catholic Church of the Good Shepherd in Beverly Hills – the same church where Dunne had been baptized 22 years earlier. Her body was laid to rest near Los Angeles, at the Westwood Memorial Park.

"An act of passion and despair."

"If (Dunne) had been killed in an automobile accident, horrible as that would have been, at least it would have been over and mourning could have begun," Dominick said. "A murder is an ongoing event until the day of the sentencing, and mourning has to be postponed."

Sweeney was charged with Dunne's murder, and the case finally went to trial at the court in Santa Monica in early August, 1983. A *People* magazine article from October 1983 described Sweeney as a "young man in a black suit" seated at a long table, his face "white as an egg" and his large, pale hands "folded meekly" over a Bible.

"It is the fashion among the criminal fraternity to find God, and Sweeney, the killer, was no exception," Dominick remembered. "The Bible was a prop; Sweeney never read it, he just rested his folded hands on it. He also wept regularly. One day, the court had to be recessed because he claimed the other prisoners had been harassing before he entered, and he needed time to cry in private.

"I could not believe that the jurors would buy such a performance."

But Sweeney painted a very different picture in the courtroom than the true colors he'd shown to Dunne's family and friends. According to Sweeney's testimony, Dunne "provoked" the violent struggle that resulted in her death, because she had previously agreed to reconcile and had then refused to take Sweeney back. Sweeney said he "just exploded and lunged toward her" after she told him she'd been lying when she said she would live with him again.

He added that he "had no memory" of the event, only that he found himself next to Dunne's unconscious body, with his hands pressed around her neck. According to Sweeney, he tried to resuscitate her, and when that didn't work, he ran into the house and swallowed two bottles of pills – attempting suicide due to his panic and regret at what he had done.

Sweeney's lawyer Michael Adelson added that Dunne was a "snob," who was constantly telling Sweeney how he was beneath her. Sweeney's account of their relationship presented Dunne as two-faced and heartless, and he said she even told him that she had been leading him on.

Dominick even recalled receiving a phone call from the prosecutor for the case, district attorney Steven Barshop, in July, shortly before the trial was set to begin. Barshop explained that Adelson had requested that Lenny not be allowed in the courtroom – Adelson felt the presence of the victim's mother, confined to a wheelchair, would create "undue sympathy for her that would be prejudicial to Sweeney."

The "accident" was a "tragedy," Adelson argued, "not a real crime – an action of passion and despair."

However, no evidence could be found to back up Sweeney's story, and investigators were reluctant to believe him. There was nothing to support Sweeney's claim that he'd attempted to commit suicide, and even during his initial interrogation, Sweeney seemed to show little remorse for his part in Dunne's death.

In fact, the police officers who arrested him testified that Sweeney had seemed "quite calm and collected," and more concerned about what would happen to him than what had happened to Dunne – only about an hour and a half after he'd been arrested.

"I fucked up, I can't believe I did something that will put me behind bars forever," Sweeney reportedly told police when he was brought down to the station. "Man, I blew it. I killed her. I didn't think I choked her that hard. I just kept on choking her. I just lost my temper and blew it again."

When one of the officers made a comment about how well Dunne had been doing with her acting career, Sweeney retorted, "well, I was doing quite well in *my* career. I'm quite proud of what I've done."

Upon further investigation, it was revealed that Sweeney had obviously strangled Dunne for about five minutes – at least four minutes, according to the medical examiner. According to police, this makes Sweeney's story fairly improbable. Not only would Sweeney have had enough time to realize what he was doing while he was choking his ex-girlfriend, he would have had the opportunity to regain control and let Dunne live.

During the trial, Dominick remembers Barshop holding up a hand to the jury, silencing the room for a four-minute period – "how long it took for Dominique Dunne to die," Barshop said, in his opening statement.

"It was horrifying," Dominick said. "I had never allowed myself to think how long she had struggled in his hands, thrashing for life. A gunshot or a knife stab is over in an instant; strangulation is an eternity."

Barshop also brought forward testimony from one of Sweeney's previous girlfriends – a secretary named Lillian Pierce, who'd also lived with Sweeney. During their relationship, which lasted from 1977 to 1980, he'd abused her on at least ten different occasions – resulting in two separate hospital visits, one for a perforated eardrum and collapsed lung, and a second time with a broken nose.

"Later, we heard that (Pierce) had sat in a car outside the church at (Dunne's) funeral and cried," Dominick said, "feeling too guilty to go inside."

The testimony proved that unlike what Sweeney's lawyer had argued, this was not a unique crime of passion, but rather a pattern of abusive behaviour toward women. Still, Sweeney's lawyer was able to convince the judge that the testimony was prejudicial, and had it excluded from the trial.

"Her account of her relationship with John Sweeney was so shocking that it should have put to rest forever the defense stand that the strangulation death of Dominique Dunne at the hands of John Sweeney was an isolated incident," wrote Dominick. "He was, it became perfectly apparent, a classic abuser of women – and his weapon was his hands."

As he questioned Pierce, without the jury present, Adelson inquired about a specific discussion the witness had had with himself and another lawyer on November 3, 1982 – the day before Dunne was officially removed from life-support and pronounced legally dead.

"Even while (Dunne) lay dying, efforts were being made to free her killer by men who knew very well that this was not his first display of violence," Dominick said. "I felt hatred for Michael Adelson. His object was to win; nothing else mattered."

Testimonies from Dunne's friends and co-workers were also ruled out after Sweeney's lawyer argued that they were nothing but hearsay. These statements explained that Dunne was not remotely interested in a reconciliation with Sweeney – in fact, she'd spent the final five weeks of her life in "permanent fear" of her abusive ex-boyfriend.

Even without this important evidence, the prosecution still sought a second-degree murder conviction, with a minimum sentence of fifteen years.

The jury did get to hear a letter found by Dunne's friends, addressed to Sweeney but obviously never sent to him. The letter detailed Dunne's frustrations at the control Sweeney attempted to hold over her, and her desire to end the relationship.

"You do not love me. You are obsessed with me. The person you think you love is not me at all. It is someone you have made up in your head," Dunne said in her letter. "I'm the person who makes you angry, who you fight with sometimes. I think we only fight when images of me fade away and you are faced with the real me.

"The whole thing has made me realize how scared I am of you, and I don't mean just physically. I'm afraid of the next time you are going to have another mood swing. When we are good, we are great. But when we are bad, we are horrendous. The bad outweighs the good."

An unsatisfying result

The trial wrapped up at the end of September, and the jury found Sweeney guilty of voluntary manslaughter – to the shock of Dunne's family and friends. "The law protected him," the jury said, but several members later admitted that had they known about Sweeney's history of violence and abuse, they would have found him guilty of the second-degree murder charge.

"I guess there is never any real satisfaction that the legal system can give, but this – the outcome – was such a blow, such a slap in the face to our family and to (Dunne's) memory," said Dunne's older brother Griffin. "They literally got away with murder... the bitterness of that will never leave."

Even Superior Court Judge Burton S. Katz, who presided over the trial, felt the system failed to provide justice for Dunne's tragic murder. Barshop stated that this failure has allowed a "time bomb" to return to the streets, where he could potentially abuse again, and blames Katz for the many rulings he made that prohibited the jury from hearing important, relevant evidence.

However, Katz argued that he had no choice but to rule the way he had – but admitted that some of the more controversial rulings during the trial "pained" him. Shortly after Sweeney's trial, Katz moved to the Juvenile Court in Sylmar.

"Nothing is more difficult than rendering a decision based upon a law with which you disagree," Katz said. "Unfortunately, following the letter of the law sometimes doesn't permit one to pursue the ultimate goal of justice."

Sweeney ended up with a sentence of only six and a half years in prison, the maximum sentence imposed for convictions of voluntary manslaughter. Instead of the fifteen years the prosecution had hoped for, Sweeney was released from a medium-security state prison after spending three years, seven months, and twenty-seven days in custody.

"Three and a half years for a life is certainly not justice," Katz said. "If I could have given him 25 (years), I would have given him 25. If I could have given him life, I would have given him life... I agree with everyone that based on his past record of violence... he is dangerous to any woman."

Soon after his release from prison, Sweeney found another high-paying job as a head chef at a chic restaurant in Santa Monica called "The Chronicle." The new position didn't last long, though -

Sweeney was fired after Dunne's family and friends descended on the restaurant with handbills that were distributed to guests and passers-by.

"The hands that prepared your food strangled Dominique Dunne on October 30, 1982," the handbills read.

Sweeney left Los Angeles for Seattle in 1989, and changed his name to John Maura. According to some sources, he is currently employed there as an executive chef for a chain restaurant.

"This guy gets to be reinstated as the head chef in a restaurant as if nothing ever happened," said Dunne's older brother, actor Griffin Dunne. "If she had lived, she'd be an actress everyone in the world would know... he's a murderer; he's murdered and I think he will do it again."

Another friend of the family echoed these thoughts, adding that "the verdict almost says it's okay to kill the one you love."

THE MURDER OF FAITH HEDGEPETH

JESSI DAVIS

Happy-go-lucky

In 1982, Connie Hedgepeth had her hands full with two teenage daughters and a husband who was addicted to drugs. Her marriage was struggling when she took a pregnancy test, hoping the result would be negative. It wasn't. Her youngest daughter was born eight months later, and Connie named her Faith.

"I felt like it was my faith in God that helped me through that situation," she said. "My faith helped me to continue to work and to do what I needed to do for my children."

Still, Connie divorced her husband when Faith was still young. Struggling to stay afloat, Connie turned to her oldest daughter, Rolanda, for support. Despite an almost 18-year age difference, Rolanda and Faith developed a strong bond – "part mother-daughter, part sister," Rolanda explained.

"We were always close. I was kind of like a second mom, but there was that sister bond, too," she said.

Rolanda's daughter Alexis was born on Faith's first birthday, and the two girls grew up together in rural North Carolina. Her upbringing was difficult, but Faith's positive attitude and eagerness to contribute propelled her through her schooling. She was an honor student, a cheerleader, and a regular volunteer for many other clubs and organizations.

"She always had this energy about her," Rolanda recalled. "She was really happy-go-lucky."

Faith's father had dropped out of college to raise his family, and Faith intended to pick up where her dad had left off. She earned a Gates Millennium Scholarship to the University of North Carolina at Chapel Hill – the very school her father had been attending. Poised to be the very first college graduate in her family, Faith had plans to become a pediatrician or a teacher once she completed her education.

Instead, the Native American biology major never made it to her 20th birthday. Police records reveal that Faith was last seen alive at approximately 3 a.m. on September 7, 2012, when she and her roommate Karena Rosario came home after an evening partying at a local nightclub.

The Thrill of a lifetime

The night before she was murdered, Faith had been studying with Karena at the Davis Library, on the university campus. At around 8 or 8:30 p.m., Faith took a break from her studies to send a text to her father – "Hey Daddy, I love you," the message read. She also texted her niece, reminding her to register to vote in the upcoming election.

At around midnight, the girls left the library and stopped back at their apartment before heading out at approximately 1 a.m. to arrive at a nightclub called The Thrill.

Just after 2:30 a.m., the girls left the bar. Karena was feeling sick after having had too much to drink, and wanted to go home. Faith helped Karena get into bed, and then fell asleep herself. However, a text message from Faith's phone was received at 3:40 a.m. by Brandon Edwards, Karena's ex-boyfriend.

"Hey b. can you come over here please," the message read. "Karena needs you more aha. You know. Please let her know you care."

A few minutes later, another text comes through that simply says, "than." It is suspected that the message was intended to fix a typo in the original message, correcting it to say "Karena needs you more *than* you know." Brandon didn't reply until the next day, when Faith's phone received a text at 4:16 p.m. that read, "Who is this?"

At around 4:30 a.m., Karena left the apartment to go over to a friend's house – and claims that she did see Faith asleep at that time. When she returned at around 11 a.m., however, she found her roommate's body in her room, in her bed, "covered by a blanket on top of her slightly askew mattress with large amounts of blood."

At 11:01 a.m., a 911 call came from the house.

Faith was unconscious and cold, Karena told the dispatcher who took the call, and there was "blood everywhere." She said she thought there may have been an altercation, explaining to the dispatcher that "there were items in the room that were not hers and that it looked like someone else had been there."

Police responded immediately, securing the scene at the girls' apartment complex and collecting evidence. They found Faith's body "positioned on the floor, leaning against the bed, with her shirt pulled up and no clothes from the waist down."

Medical examiners concluded that the cause of death was blunt force trauma, based on the severe beating Faith had endured. When the autopsy report was unsealed nearly two years after the killing, it was revealed that she also had bruises and cuts all over her arms and legs, as well as blood underneath her fingernails.

"It's very, very hard, learning of how Faith died," said Rolanda. "She was beaten, she was bludgeoned to death. A lot of people don't understand what that means, but it was really bad."

A rape kit had also been performed, indicating the presence of semen – with DNA that matched other DNA that police had recovered at the scene. Law enforcement officials have not confirmed whether the sexual activity was consensual or forced.

Searching for suspects

In the years since Faith's death, multiple search warrants have been executed – as well as numerous court orders for things like cell phones, computers, and even social media accounts. DNA testing has also been carried out on many of men that interacted with Karena and Faith while they were at the nightclub, but so far, investigators have found no matching results.

While at The Thrill, Faith was reportedly dancing with a man named David Bell. He told police he didn't know Faith very well, and was not named by police as a suspect during the investigation.

"(Redacted) was identified as walking out of Club Thrill with Faith Hedgepeth shortly before the homicide occurred," read a police report unsealed in 2014. "He was the last male to be seen with her before her death."

The report added that Bell admitted to talking with Faith the night she was killed, and to meeting her the weekend before. He refused to provide investigators with a sample of his DNA, claiming that he had likely touched her at some point during the night of the homicide. His statements to law enforcement officers were also determined to be "inconsistent" with statements provided by others.

Another man, Jacob Beatley, was interviewed by police and also not named as a suspect. Karena visited him during the early morning hours of September 7, after leaving the apartment she shared with Faith. DNA was also sought from a man named Reginald Leonard Jackson II, who was not named as a suspect despite having been texting regularly with Faith in the days prior to her murder.

However, none of this information was offered to Faith's family until the documents were unsealed in 2014.

"All they have said to us and to the public, to the media, to everybody, (is) that this wasn't random – how do they know that?" said Chad Hedgepeth, Faith's brother. "Do they have a suspect? Do they have any suspects? … Tell us something, because being in the dark on any and everything these past four weeks has been brutal."

While the recording from the 911 call seems to indicate that Karena was alone when she discovered Faith's body in their apartment, the police report stated that she returned to their home with a friend. In the recording, however, Karena consistently claims "I just walked into my apartment," instead of saying "we." There is also no sound recorded that could be attributed to another person in the room.

An analysis of the call could suggest that the repetition of the statement "I just walked into my apartment" is an attempt to establish an alibi – especially since the recording reveals that Karena says this several times before even providing the dispatcher with necessary information like the victim's state or the location of the emergency.

At no point in the call does Karena specifically ask for help for the victim. She also apologizes to the dispatcher, using language that analysts typically see in calls where guilty knowledge is indicated.

Initially, law enforcement turned their attention to Eriq Takoy Jones – an ex-boyfriend of Karena's who lived in the same apartment complex and was reportedly an aspiring rapper. Just a few months before the murder, Karena had filed a restraining order against Eriq, on the basis of domestic assault. Police had previously investigated claims that Eriq had kicked two of the doors in the girls' apartment completely off their frames, and eyewitness accounts reported that Karena had been seen with visible injuries to her body – inflicted, she said, by her ex-boyfriend.

"Faith took Karena to take out a restraining order," said Faith's father, Roland Hedgepeth. "I think that very possibly, Takoy may have had some ill feelings toward Faith for doing that."

Rolanda said Faith had moved in with Karena after the restraining order had been filed, to help her friend as she recovered from the abusive relationship.

"I wasn't worried about Faith at the time," Rolanda said. "I wanted them to be safe. I just wanted both of them to be safe."

Just before Faith was murdered, Eriq posted a chilling message on his Facebook page, and texted a similar message to an acquaintance.

"Deal Lord," the post read. "Forgive me for all of my sins and the sins I may commit today. Protect me from the girls who don't deserve me and the ones who wish me dead today."

An unnamed person who claimed to be a former roommate of Faith's called the Chapel Hill Police Department the day after Faith's body was discovered with additional concerning information about Eriq. According to the caller, Faith had told her that Karena's boyfriend hated her (Faith) and told her that if Karena wouldn't get back together with him, he would kill Faith.

However, Eriq was very cooperative with law enforcement during the investigation into Faith's murder. Both his apartment and car were combed for trace evidence, and his DNA was tested and cleared.

"From what I knew of her (Faith), she was the sweetest person in the world. If you needed her and she could do it, she was there," Eriq told news reporters after Faith's murder. "I'll be honest with you – whoever did this deserves to burn."

Investigators also learned that the ex-boyfriend of Karena's that Faith had texted in the hours before she was killed had also been present that night at The Thrill. Police records indicated that Brandon Edwards had even spent the night at the girls' apartment the night before the murder – making his response to Faith's texts the day she was killed quite unusual.

According to a friend named Marisol Rangel, Karena and Brandon were "just friends" at the time of Faith's murder. Marisol is the friend who was reportedly with Karena when she discovered Faith's body, but the 911 operator was confident that Karena was alone when the call was placed.

In January 2013, police released a profile of the killer. According to the profile, developed by Chapel Hill Police and the FBI's Behavioral Analysis Unit, the person responsible for Faith's murder might have been familiar with her – and possibly even lived near her in the past.

The individual may have also "made comments" about Faith in the past, with their behavior shifting after the murder occurred. Obviously, the profile indicated this person would have been "unaccounted for" during the early morning hours of September 7, 2012. Police also stated the DNA evidence collected at the scene of the homicide points toward a "male suspect."

At the time, Faith's father Roland said the development of the profile marked a "new beginning" in the investigation, and believed it would help police solve the case.

"For us, we're kind of stuck back on September 7," he said. "Every day, we get up and relive that day. But I'm confident things will open up soon."

Strange evidence

Nearly two years after the murder, police released a shocking and mysterious piece of evidence. A spiteful, handwritten note was found scrawled on a fast food bag left near the crime scene, with the words "I'M NOT STUPID BITCH JEALOUS."

Police believe the note was written by the killer, but have not said whether the handwriting has ever been officially analyzed. According to private investigator and forensic handwriting examiner Peggy Walla, some clues can be determined from the note.

"What struck me was how clean the document is – the crime scene was pretty bloody, and there's nothing on this document," she said. "Looking at it, I would get the impression it was either written outside of the crime scene, or it was written before, like a premeditation."

She also feels the words were written by a non-dominant hand, indicating that whoever wrote the note was attempting to "disguise" their penmanship. The block letters could be taken as the writer's attempt to distance themselves from authority, she said.

"The word and sentence phrase 'I'm not stupid' is a hot push-button factor," Walla added. "That's probably the most important thing said. This was a jealous person who was called 'stupid.' The person that said it who is now deceased has no way of repeating this person is stupid, which is another way to shut them up."

Users of online forums have also speculated that the use of the word 'jealous' could indicate that the writer of the note was a woman, as the word is thought to be more frequently used by females. The formation of the letter 'P' in particular has also struck some as seeming feminine in nature.

Other speculation surrounds the intent of the note. The words 'jealous' and 'bitch' suggest that the note was not meant for the police of for the public – rather, these deeply personal words were likely intended toward Faith, or possibly even Karena, who would eventually find the body. But more curious yet is the situation that must have occurred that led to the writing of the note. What happened before Faith was murdered?

Cries for help

A clue may be found in a voicemail left for a friend the night of her death. The call appears to have been a pocket-dial – a very timely pocket-dial that potentially recorded the final minutes of Faith's life. The timestamp on the nearly unintelligible message indicates that the call was made while Faith was still at The Thrill, but some have argued that a glitch in technology could have resulted in an incorrect time.

According to President and CEO of Creative Forensic Services Arlo West, who is certified by the New York Institute of Forensic Audio in enhancement, authentication, and analysis of both audio and video, the names 'Rosie' and 'Eriq' appear throughout the recording – potentially referring to Karena Rosario and her ex-boyfriend Eriq Takoy Jones.

"I've worked on hundreds, if not thousands, of cases where people have pocket-dialed somebody," West said. "If you can peel back those layers of noise, you start to get a better picture of the dialogue that is contained – stuff that starts to make a little more sense."

In his analysis for Crime Watch Daily, West identified two distinct female voices – one which he claimed is Faith Hedgepeth, and the other he describes as a "very angry female." He also picked out at least two male voices.

"I hear what I believe is Miss Hedgepeth's cries for help," West said. "You can hear her emotive voice, the tone of her voice, is clearly in pain ... You can clearly hear what I believe is Faith pleading. She's being hurt, being attacked."

West said he feels "very confident" about hearing the names 'Rosie' and 'Eriq,' and included both names in his transcript of the three-minute recording.

He also claims iPhones were "inherently problematic with timestamping" during the time Faith was killed – which he said accounts for the timestamp on the voicemail showing 1:23 a.m., while police believe Faith was killed sometime after 4:30 a.m. Still, Chapel Hill police did contact West for an official analysis of the recording.

"If it is Faith being murdered, and captured in this recording – which I think it is, this is pivotal," West said. "It should be able to solve this case."

Police seem to believe that the voicemail was recorded from the club, not from the apartment – and in the middle of the call, there appears to be music playing or someone rapping. There is also no evidence to support that the name 'Rosie' could have referred to Karena, and Eriq Takoy Jones was apparently called 'Takoy' by his friends.

Still, the voicemail is difficult to discount – especially since, on the night Faith was murdered, it appears to have recorded an emotionally-charged, angry discussion. To many listeners, including members of Faith's family, the voices sound agitated – belligerent, fast-speaking – and seem to be punctuated by audible yelps of what could be pain.

"From day one, I heard my daughter screaming in the background," said Faith's father, Roland. "I knew something was going on."

"A really good case."

The note, the voicemail audio, and other documents – including the 15-page autopsy – were unsealed in September 2014. According to Chris Blue, Chapel Hill Police Chief, the effort was an attempt to generate new leads in the investigation.

"We have excellent evidence – we have a really good case," he said. "We just need to connect this really good case with the killer."

However, in those two years, police had been unable to connect any potential suspect with the crime. The official documents were sealed during that time despite repeated requests from lawyers and news organizations to open them to the public, as investigators felt releasing the information would compromise their efforts.

"It's not that it might hinder this investigation, it will hinder this investigation," said Durham County Assistant District Attorney Charlene Franks.

She added that details contained within the documents, including the 911 call where the crime scene and body are vividly described, could help police identify the killer – as that information would have been known by very few people.

In a "cold case," Franks said, police will often turn to the public for assistance. However, since the investigation into Faith's murder is ongoing, solving the case means keeping the public – including Faith's family – in the dark about some vital details.

"The most important thing to them and the state and the Chapel Hill Police Department is to find the killer of their baby girl, Faith Hedgepeth," she said. "The only way to do that is to keep those items sealed because the information contained in there, other than (investigators), only the killer knows."

According to Steve Hale, private investigator and retired homicide detective who was never involved with the case, it's typical for law enforcement to keep the details of a case under wraps – interviews and tips that haven't been influenced by media reports can make or break a case.

"If there is a suspect, he may not know he's a suspect, and they're waiting for him to get careless and maybe make a comment to an accessory after the fact," he said, adding that detectives likely suspected someone who knew Faith and might have had a distinct motive.

Each document pertaining to the case was reviewed by Judge Howard Manning before being unsealed in 2014. Still, three investigators with the Chapel Hill Police Department and State Bureau of Investigation continued working exclusively on the unsolved case – and offered a reward of $40,000 for any information leading to the arrest and conviction of Faith's killer.

"We really want to bring some peace to Faith's family," said Blue. "This has been two unimaginable years for them."

"Your imagination starts to run wild."

Connie was contacted three hours after Faith's body was found, by a crisis counselor who told her little more than that her 19-year-old daughter Faith had been found dead in her apartment – the victim of what appeared to be a violent homicide.

"I said, 'you must have the wrong girl,'" Connie remembers. "She told me it was her, and I said, 'I don't think so.'"

It fell on Connie to contact the rest of the family, spreading the devastating news to her son, her ex-husband, and her eldest daughter, Rolanda. At that point, Connie said, she didn't have much to tell them other than that Faith was dead.

"They couldn't tell us very much because they didn't want to jeopardize the investigation," she explained. "Not knowing anything at all... your imagination starts to run wild."

Even after detectives brought the family to Chapel Hill, about 80 miles away from their home in Hollister, Connie still had no answers to her many questions. She wasn't even permitted to visit the crime scene, or see her youngest daughter.

"I just wanted to hold her hand, to let her know I was there," Connie recalled. "I still cry for my baby, and I wonder if she called out for help. Did she cry for me? These are the things you think."

Finally, the family was told the cause of death – but without any kind of motive or indication of what could have happened to lead up to Faith's murder, the new information was difficult for the family to process.

"It is getting harder, not knowing what happened, trying to accept what happened," said Rolanda. "She was beautiful. She didn't deserve it. She had a lot going for her."

While no arrests have been made, and no suspects even identified, Chapel Hill Police Lt. Josh Mecimore said police are still confident that the killer will be found and brought to justice.

"Someone knows something, and we're continually appealing to the public to come forward," he said. "This is not a cold case. We are still following up on things, still pounding the pavement, still waiting for that one piece of evidence that will help us solve this case."

Connie, Rolanda, and the rest of the Hedgepeth family are clinging to the same hope.

"At some point, God will let us know what happened," Rolanda said. "Even when I'm down, I still believe that we will find that person."

However, neighbours remain concerned as a result of the limited information available – and the fact that police have yet to make an arrest. While law enforcement officers continued to reassure nearby residents that the incident was an isolated event, neighbours wanted more answers.

"It's not a reassuring thought to wonder if you can send your kids to safety to the bus stop or if something could happen," said Anna Salomon, who lived with her husband and children in the subdivision next to the apartment complex where Faith was murdered. In the weeks following the killing, the neighbours banded together to walk children to the bus stop in collective groups.

Keeping Faith alive

One year after Faith was killed, students at the University of North Carolina gathered on campus at the Bell Tower Amphitheatre for a silent walk in celebration of the student's life. She was also made an honorary member of the Alpha Pi Omega Sorority, the country's oldest Native American Greek letter organization.

"She was the happiest person I knew, always laughing, always smiling," said Faith's friend Leslie Locklear.

Another friend, Victoria Chavis, remembered Faith's "bubbly personality."

"She had a smile that was just infectious," she said, "and she was a wonderful person to be around."

"The entire Carolina community grieves for the loss of this promising, vibrant student," added UNC Chancellor Carol Folt.

The family has honored Faith's memory by establishing the "Faith's Smile Scholarship" in her name – an award which will go to Native American women entering their freshman year of college. The scholarship project gives the family something positive to focus on while they continue searching for answers.

"It's really hard – hard because of not knowing what happened and not knowing why it happened, who did it," Rolanda added. "One little piece of information could break the case, could give us some type of peace. How could somebody withhold that, after everything we have lost?"

Still, for Connie, nothing can extinguish the shining light that defined her youngest daughter, Faith – no matter how many years go by with the case remaining unsolved.

"We don't want anyone to forget her smile. She was a beautiful girl, she was my baby," Connie said. "Her spirit is right here today."

IRA YARMOLENKO

On a seemingly normal Thursday afternoon on the Catawba River in May of 2008, two jet skiers planned on having a picnic together along the river when they stumbled upon a peculiar sight that would change their lives forever - a car crashed into a stump on the banks of the river along with the horrifying sight of a dead body lying next to it. They quickly alerted authorities and soon discovered that the body was that of a deceased young woman.

This was the tragic fate of Irina "Ira" Yarmolenko, a University of North Carolina college student who had just celebrated her twentieth birthday several days earlier. She was discovered with three items from her car tied around her neck. There was no sign of a struggle or any clear indication of a motive. She was not sexually assaulted or robbed.

Although first responders initially thought her death could have been a suicide, her death was ruled a homicide by asphyxiation. To this day, her murder still garners interest from the public due to the strange yet disturbing circumstances surrounding her death. Add to that the whispers that surround the case about the possibility that her convicted murderer, Mark Carver, might actually be an innocent man. What followed this horrific discovery was an investigation into the crime scene and into her personal life to uncover what happened to Ira.

Ira's early life and college experience

Ira Yarmolenko was born in the Ukraine on May 2nd, 1988 but emigrated to the United States when she was eight, along with her parents and brother Pavel. The family reportedly fled the Ukraine as refugees due to religious persecution. Her parents, both research scientists, were able to find job opportunities in North Carolina.

Ira quickly picked up the language and by all accounts seemed to assimilate well into American culture. She lived in North Carolina for most of her life, spoke with a southern accent and had several personal interests. Like most teenagers, she enjoyed hiking, acting, photography, sports, and music.

She also played the piano and liked listening to bands, such as the Counting Crows. She was also extremely academic. She excelled in math and science while being an active member of her high school poetry team. Ira was especially close to her family. Although she left Chapel Hill for UNC Charlotte, about a 3-hour drive away, she spoke to her mother almost every day. After her death, her mother said to reporters, "I don't think what I'm living is called life anymore."

During her two years in college, she found other interests beyond her required coursework at UNC Charlotte, where she was an undeclared major but had a strong interest in French. She was a photographer for the University Times, her college paper, and occasionally wrote columns and articles for the Niner Online, an online student-run newspaper.

She was also a member of the university's Russian Club as Russian was her first language. Her Russian language classmate described her as, "the kind of girl that always made you feel special, wanted, needed, cared for, and loved. It always seemed like she was always so happy to see you, and would always take at least a second of her time to say hello to you." It was here that she met her roommate Masha, another student from the Ukraine.

Masha and Ira bonded over the fact that they both spoke Russian and came from similar backgrounds. Masha described the day that she found out Ira was murdered when two investigators showed up at the small apartment that she shared with Ira, "It was her student I.D. picture. And I just started screaming. Sorry. Both of our families immigrated here to this country for a better life and sacrificed so much." Like most people close to Ira, Masha was devastated to hear the news of her friend's death.

Most people who knew Ira described her as outgoing. They felt that she would not have been afraid if a stranger had approached her. She was involved on campus and worked at a local coffee shop, Jackson's Java. Years after her death, her picture could still be found on the counter of Jackson's Java. She had a lasting impact on those that knew her. Her brother said, "Everything that she's ever done was to help people."

At UNC Charlotte, she had many close friends and acquaintances who described her as a cheerful and bubbly person, yet still high-achieving. In addition to her job at the coffee shop, Ira also worked as an aid in a computer lab on campus. The week before finals, her roommate Masha and friends threw a party for her 20th birthday.

During this party, her friends reported that Ira ended up cooking for everyone there, despite the fact that party was a celebration in her honor. This was not uncommon for her to do and was just the kind of person she was. Her friends concluded the celebration by visiting an art exhibit. They reported that she was in good spirits and that they parted amicably.

Although it seemed Ira was thriving in her environment at UNC Charlotte, she was in the process of closing her chapter there and beginning a new one at UNC-Chapel Hill, a school a bit closer to home. "Ira indicated she was sad to leave her friends behind at UNCC, but she was looking forward to attending UNC-Chapel Hill in the fall," according to Sgt. Tindall, an investigator in the case.

She had resigned from her positions at the coffee shop and in the computer lab where she had worked during her sophomore year shortly before she was murdered. Her brother Pavel, a then Ph.D. graduate student at Duke said, "She was not sure how she felt about leaving Charlotte. But she was very, very excited about coming to Chapel Hill."

Ira intended on transferring to UNC-Chapel Hill to be closer to her family and to major in public health. The day of her murder, she visited the coffee shop and said goodbye to her friends there and left a gift, a book, for her former boss. She also took several items to the

Goodwill to donate and visited her credit union where she deposited some checks before heading to the river about 20 miles away.

The scene of the crime

The Catawba River is over 200 miles long and spans two states. It is located about 20 minutes from Charlotte and is popular among fisherman, boaters and jet skiers. First responders on that fateful day described a perplexing, yet disturbing scene.

The doors on the driver's side of Ira's car were opened, and her body was found just a few feet away. It did not appear she was sexually assaulted or robbed, nor did she have defensive wounds from fighting off her attacker or attackers.

Three ligatures were found around her neck: a nylon ribbon from a bag in her car, a drawstring from the hood of a jacket and a bungee cord. The drawstring was wrapped around her neck. The ribbon was wrapped once around her neck and oddly tied in a bow in the front. Her hair and body were also wet, although she was found on dry ground.

According to Detective Terry during the trial, "Her head was back towards the embankment. Her feet were near the river underneath some brush. Upon closer inspection, she was actually holding some of that brush in her hand. . . ." It was determined that this was the place where she was murdered and that she had not been transferred there.

Investigators began piecing together her movements before arriving at the river banks and determined it was likely that she headed down to the river banks to take pictures, as she was an avid photographer. Her brother Pavel said he "wasn't surprised she would go to such a remote spot. She was adventurous. She once hiked the Stampede Trail in Alaska with friends, searching for an abandoned bus made famous by Jon Krakauer's book Into the Wild."

Her camera was found in the trunk of her car, but there was not any film in it that could yield any clues about her death. Investigators quickly began interviewing people along the river to see if anyone had heard or seen anything out of the ordinary and came across two fishermen who were fishing about 100 yards from where Ira's body and car were discovered.

Mark Carver and Neil Cassada were cousins who grew up in the area and had been fishing in a new spot they had discovered the weekend before. This spot was about 100 yards from where Ira's car and body were discovered. Carver had been excited about the spot. He had returned to it because it did not require him to haul his boat to the river which was difficult for Carver to do since he suffers from carpal tunnel syndrome, a condition that makes his hands extremely weak.

His doctors recommended he not lift anything heavier than five pounds. Cassada also suffered from a heart condition, making it difficult to do anything too physical. Investigators questioned both men who reported that they had not seen Ira or had not heard anything from their fishing spot. They did report hearing a scraping sound that sounded like noise from construction.

They both willingly provided their DNA to investigators and went on their way. With the lack of forensic clues pointing toward any viable suspects, it was not until forensic analysis of the car several months later revealed partial DNA matches for Carver and Cassada that they became the prime suspects for Ira's murder. Mark Carver and Neal Cassada were arrested in December of 2008, seven months after her death and charged with conspiracy and murder. A day before Cassada's the trial began in 2010, Cassada died of a heart attack. Carver has always proclaimed their innocence.

"Simple" life of Mark Carver

Simple is the word often used to describe Mark Carver. "Simple in his routine, simple in his thought process, simple in his desires and wants," defense attorney Brent Ratchford said to reporters. Unlike Ira, Carver is not well-educated and has limitations with writing and reading comprehension, which he has struggled with throughout most of his life.

At an early age, he was placed in special education classes because of these limitations and his relatively low IQ. At 16, he dropped out of school to work in a mill. At the time he was arrested, it was documented that he was taking medication prescribed for schizophrenia.

Carver is also the father of four children from two different marriages. "He lived for his children and family," his sister-in-law Robin Carver said when asked about him. "He didn't really do much of anything else. Fishing and hunting and family, that was about it."

Although his family speaks well of Carver, like most family members often do, he did have prior brushes with the law despite never being convicted of a crime. In 2005, Carver faced a charge of injury to property. Carver purportedly confronted two people he thought were stealing his four-wheeler. The charge was dismissed, and the file no longer exists. A year before Ira's murder, Carver accidentally shot his son. Carver and his son were supposedly wrestling when the gun went off. "It was an accident," his son said. The case was later dismissed and Carver never convicted of a crime.

Cassada also had had his own dealings with the law. In 1995, he was accused of assault and injury to personal property. He reportedly pointed a gun at someone. But the charges were dismissed and the details remain unclear.

His family insists that he had nothing to do with Ira's murder and that the stress of the trial for a crime he did not commit ultimately led to his death. Kaye Cassada, Neal Cassada's wife said "After 37 years of loving that man and being married to that man, I know he is not capable of hurting anybody. He would have died to help somebody." Charges against Cassada were dropped, a common proceeding with deceased suspects. His family attended the hearing and his son Shannon Cassada said, "We want everybody to hear that he was an innocent man."

Carver also maintains his own innocence, stating "they said that they had ... my DNA and Neal's DNA in the car. I know that's a lie because Neal left, and they couldn't have gotten no DNA because I wasn't down there. I didn't go around it. I didn't go around the car. You know what I'm saying?" He also said he didn't think Cassada would commit such a crime because "He's got four young'uns himself."

Although lie detector tests are not reliable enough to be used in court, during the initial investigation Cassada took a polygraph test, which he passed. Because he passed, investigators did not give Carver one. Carver has been very vocal about his willingness to also take a polygraph test.

Touch DNA

During the investigation and trial, Carver never wavered in proclaiming his innocence and said this to Ira's family "I never seen her that day. If I'd knowed she was up there, I would have went up there and helped her. They could have easily come down and killed me just like they did her."

His trial began in 2010. Before the trial, Carver was offered a surprising plea deal from the prosecution: 4-8 years in prison if he pleaded guilty to second degree murder. Had he taken this deal and pled guilty to murder he could be out of prison and with his family. His attorney said, "I have never gotten such a low offer. And to me that spoke volumes about the case." Carver turned down this offer and prosecutors moved forward with the case.

Prosecutors argued that the two men killed Ira because she witnessed or photographed something they did not want her to see. As a result, they strangled her and pushed her car on the embankment where their DNA was transferred to the car. Their intention was to sink the car in the water, but it hit a stump where it stayed until it was finally discovered by the jet skiers. They then returned to their fishing spot until they were questioned by police.

Prosecutors relied on a relatively new forensic technique at the time known as "touch DNA." Unlike previous methods, touch DNA uses smaller amounts of DNA, such as skin cells transferred to a person or object when they come into contact with someone. But touch DNA is not as reliable as other DNA methods requiring blood or saliva because it is difficult to determine the origin of these cells. For instance, skin cells can be transferred indirectly by a third party or carrier.

For example, a man in California was falsely imprisoned because his DNA was found on a murder victim. It was determined that it was impossible that he was a killer because he had a solid alibi. At the time of the murder, he was unconscious in a hospital due to extreme intoxication.

Prosecutors then discovered that the same paramedic who treated him for intoxication was a first responder at the murder scene. The DNA from the intoxicated man was presumably transferred to the victim by the paramedic. This case set a precedent about the reliability of touch DNA and is cited by Carver's advocates for innocence as a possibility as to why Carver's and Cassada's DNA was found on Ira's car.

Despite this interesting theory, it was not presented by the defense in Carver's trial and the jury found him guilty of murder. He was sentenced to and is currently serving life in prison. Carver's advocates argue that the car and crime scene was not preserved, and that Carver and Cassada's DNA could have been transferred by officers or other people near the crime scene. Many officers, the jet skiers, first responders were all present at the crime scene and could have all inadvertently transferred the DNA to the car.

Several other inconsistencies exist in the prosecution's case. Carvers DNA was not found on her body nor on the trunk of the car where he and Cassada would have pushed it into the river bank according to prosecutors. Carvers DNA did not match a third DNA profile found on the bungee cord and the only DNA found under Ira's fingernails was her own.

His attorney and advocates also argue that the two men couldn't have physically pushed the car into the river bank due to Carver's carpal tunnel and Cassada's heart condition. Cassada supposedly got winded just walking. In 2013, Carver's attorneys filed an appeal on his behalf, but the appeals court determined "no error in the defendant's trial" occurred, meaning his conviction of life in prison would be upheld. But this did not deter his advocates from trying to prove Carver did not receive a fair defense during his trial.

Earlier this year, a judge granted the request of the North Carolina Actual Innocence Project, attorneys who have become interested in Carver case who believe Carver is wrongfully imprisoned, to see DNA reports that were never shared with Carvers defense team, along with further DNA testing.

They argue that Carver did not receive a proper defense as his lawyers did not call any witnesses or DNA experts to the stand and address the DNA evidence, and that the DNA evidence is not compelling enough beyond a reasonable doubt to warrant a life sentence for Carver. It is the only evidence linking Carver to the crime. Only time will determine the final outcomes of Carver's appeals as the evidentiary hearing has been postponed. Legal proceedings could take several years.

Other suspects

If Carver and Cassada's DNA was indeed transferred by a third party and they did not kill Ira, then who did? There was no one in her life that seemed to have any motive. Besides these two men, there was only one other suspect in her murder investigation. Nine months after the murder, Christopher Lemont Cooper wrote a letter to News anchor Erica Bryant to "confess a sin," that he and several other accomplices had killed Ira.

He said he drove a van full of friends that were all high and needed money for drugs. He said he was unable to sleep "because of what we did to that young woman." And wished to meet with the reporter. The TV station did not publish the letter and turned it over to investigators where they took the letter very seriously and launched an investigation with the North Carolina State Bureau of Investigations.

Police and investigators visited Cooper, where he was in jail on charges of rape, assault by strangulation, and for being delinquent in child support. He reportedly refused to cooperate with investigators, but they ultimately ruled him out as a suspect concluding that several of the accomplices he named were incarcerated at the time of the murder. They also cleared the other accomplices named in Cooper's letter and continued building their case against Carver and Cassada.

Free Mark Carver

Free Mark Carver is one of the prominent websites advocating for the release of Carver. They believe he is innocent or at the very least did not receive a proper defense in his trial. The website is run by a former newspaper journalist who now works in the fashion industry. She had no ties to the case or families and became intrigued with the case in 2011 after its details aired on Dateline NBC and through other online news articles.

One of the major theories from Carver's advocates presented on the website is that Ira was not murdered and in fact committed suicide by placing the ligatures around her neck herself. They claim that Ira was not the cheerful person described by her friends and loved ones and that she had battled depression.

Her boyfriend had broken up with her shortly before her murder and her poetry was sometimes dark and melancholy. The website alludes to accounts from unnamed people who claim that Ira had attempted suicide when she was younger and had seen a therapist at UNC Charlotte. The website does not provide sources and only mentions them as letters to the author.

Although this theory may be offensive to those who loved Ira and describe her as a happy and vibrant young woman, it has been addressed by pathologists who have dismissed this theory saying "For this to have been anything but a homicide, i.e., this was a suicide, this victim would have to tie three ligatures around her neck tightly and before death get into this position while that's going on and her legs underneath the brush given that position and I just feel like that was not consistent with what we are seeing. . . . Yes, and another thing that this illustrates a little bit better also is the presence of particular matter, soil and grass on her skirt as well. So that's another thing that would have had to happen. If this was a suicide she would have had to do all this stuff by herself. It is just not consistent with that theory."

Her brother Pavel, who has since completed his Ph.D. in biomedical engineering and continues to conduct research at a pediatric hospital, said he has read some of the internet theories about his sister's death, but they are "not grounded in reality." He asserts that his sister never attempted suicide and there was no indication she was depressed. Nevertheless, the fact remains that a lively, young woman lost her life just days after her 20th birthday.

Memorials

We may never know what really happened to Ira or why someone chose to take her life but it is clear that she touched many people who strive to keep her memory alive. The jet skiers who found her body, Dennis Lovelace and Brenda Pierce, placed a memorial cross where they found her car. The changing levels of the Catawba river sometimes covers part of the cross, but it is still visible to visitors.

A memorial bench as far as Alaska, where Ira spent a summer waitressing, also bears her name. "A Kansas City based artist Shane Blindt designed and installed this bench at the request of many co-workers whose lives were touched with Ira's presence during the 2007 McKinley Village Lodge summer season. Lettering on the memorial was hand drawn with pen showing the elegance and beauty of Ira's outward expressions contrasted with a raw and rugged placement into the world she left behind." It is maintained by locals there.

Her high school poetry team in Chapel Hill renamed the group The Sacrificial Poets in her honor.

What Time Devours is a book written by her former professor at UNC Charlotte who dedicated his book to her memory. He directed a campus production, which Ira was a part of the previous year before she was murdered. He also included a line from her poetry and her picture in the dedication of the book.

The controversy around her murder continues to intrigue people and several websites and pages are dedicated to outlining the details of the case. Ira's murder has been featured on Dateline and 20/20. She continues to captivate an almost cult following, and many people are still tirelessly working to prove that Carver is innocent and did not receive a fair trial. If this is the case, it means that justice has not been served for Ira and her family. But one thing is for sure, the memory of Ira Yarmolenko will continue to live on with her family, friends, and strangers that have been touched by her story.

www.ingramcontent.com/pod-product-compliance
Lightning Source LLC
Chambersburg PA
CBHW031425150726

47989CB00002B/803